DAVID'S SONG

THE AMAZING SECRET OF PSALM 23

by

Maurice Berquist

Reformation Publishers
Clarksville, Tennessee

Reformation Publishers, Inc..
242 University Drive
Prestonsburg, KY 41653

Orders 1-800-765-2464
Information 606-886-7222
Fax 606-886-8222
rpublisher@aol.com
www.reformationpublishers.com

Reformation Publishers 2006
Printed in the United States of America

David's Song:

The Amazing Secret of Psalm 23

by Maurice Berquist

Published by
Warner Press, Inc.
Anderson, Indiana

Dedicated
to
Mary and Joe Minkler of
Pasadena, California, and all
their friends who also would
like to dedicate a book to them.

*The Good Shepherd
will lead you to a
discovery of yourself
and of the person
you can become.*

—Maurice Berquist

Contents

Chapter 1:

How Much Is
a Song Worth?

It pays to sing. If you sing, I want to give you a new song; if you don't sing, I want to get you started.

In Honolulu, Hawaii, Julio Iglesias is scheduled to sing for a New Year's Eve celebration. According to the newspaper, tickets for this performance are one hundred dollars apiece. The singer explains that usually tickets cost much more, but he particularly likes to spend New Year's Eve in Honolulu. "It is lucky for me," he says.

Tickets to one of Julio's concerts have sold for as much as two thousand dollars.

Maybe there is more to music than we thought!

In 1704, Andrew Fletcher wrote:

1

> If a man were permitted to make all the ballads, he
> need not care who should make the laws of a nation.

Fletcher wrote this before the Declaration of Independence or the Constitution of the United States were formed. Few laws existed on the books of this new land. Songs there were.

Music has always mingled with the cries of prisoners. In biblical times, sunburned slaves sang as they toiled under the long whips of their Egyptian guards. Desert winds and sand have smoothed the surfaces of the pyramids. The kings are gone. Songs that echoed against the giant blocks of stone are still alive. And the nation that sang is still alive. In the cotton fields of the American south before the civil war, songs made the heat and hurt bearable. From the prisons of pain have come some of our sweetest songs.

But music is more than a comfort. It is power, power we all need.

For most of us, the story of the Hebrew captives toiling under the lash of pharaoh's taskmasters is ancient history. Nothing more. Our ancestors may have bent their backs in the cotton fields, but we live in a polyester world where people bend their backs only to the rhythms of video-taped exercise programs.

We are free people. Not prisoners. Of course, if we remember the poet's words,

> Stone walls do not a prison make
> Nor iron bars a cage,

we might see ourselves differently. Maybe we are prisoners, prisoners of sickness, stress, despair, circumstances. Even memory. Anytime we say, "I would love to do something, but I cannot because—," we are admitting our captivity.

We need a song to set us free.

Who shall write such a song? Are we brave enough to sing it? Are we alert enough to recognize it?

Not long ago a friend called me greatly disturbed. As a long-standing member of a vigorous congregation, he had always exercised a significant influence on the program. But now he had a serious complaint.

"What seems to be wrong?" I asked.

2

"It's our pastor. He has started so many new things that I don't feel at home anymore."

"Is the church losing people because of these new things?" I asked.

"On the contrary. We seem to be reaching new people all the time."

"Then," I asked, "why are you unhappy?"

"It's the music. Our pastor doesn't use the old songs of the church, the ones I grew up with. Instead he has all kinds of new songs and choruses. Scriptures. The psalms. And I don't like it."

"I understand your problem," I told him. "I know how you feel."

Truthfully, I do understand and I do know how he feels. I grew up with the songs of John and Charles Wesley, Fanny Crosby, P.P. Bliss, and D.S. Warner. These were the "old" songs. Written in the last part of the nineteenth century and the first part of the twentieth, these were the heritage songs. I know them. And I love them.

But these are not the songs that Jesus sang when he worshiped in the synagogue. Strange to say, those century-old songs are the new ones. They are not the songs that the Hebrews chanted as they made mud bricks under Egypt's blistering sun.

Interesting, even laughable, that we should have forgotten. The Scriptures set to music is not new. They are the old songs. Psalms especially were written to be sung. Even in the twentieth century. Even by people who resent their "newness" as they long for the tunes of their childhood.

The psalms are songs of power. Strange power. Almost incredible power.

Let me tell you two fascinating stories that hint at this power, this magic of songs.

Chapter 2:

An After-Hours Concert

Grizzled prisoners stirred uneasily as they were awakened by music. Sitting upright on their cushionless beds, they strained to hear the sound that had awakened them. Music. A song. Impossible as it sounded, music was indeed creeping through the cracks of the stone walls of the prison.

Accustomed to the raw life of a Roman prison, these men had learned to sleep through every kind of noise. Curses, shouts, screams, and crying. Rattling chains and cracking whips no longer disturbed them. But music, flowing like a perfumed breeze over the jagged rocks, awakened them.

Who would sing in a prison? What were they singing? And, most difficult of all, why?

5

To the uneducated ears of the prisoners in the Roman colony of Philippi, the words were unclear. A Hebrew chant, no doubt. Strange. Beautiful. But why would anyone sing at midnight? Had someone come to set them free? Or were they finally driven insane? Rome had written the laws, but David had written the song. Two men with bleeding naked backs and with feet fastened in blocks of wood to keep them from escaping either the prison or the discomfort of the cold stone floor—these men were singing. In defiance of Rome's law, the song of the prisoners echoed through the jail.

What came of all this madness? Let the historian, Luke, tell the story in his own words:

> The crowd joined in the attack against Paul and Silas. Then the officials tore the clothes off Paul and Silas, and ordered them to be whipped. After a severe beating, they were thrown into jail, and the jailer was ordered to lock them up tight. Upon receiving this order, the jailer threw them into the inner cell and fastened their feet between heavy blocks of wood. About midnight Paul and Silas were praying and singing hymns to God, and the other prisoners were listening to them. Suddenly there was a violent earthquake, which shook the prison to its foundations. At once all the doors were opened, and the chains fell off all the prisoners (Acts 16:22-26, TEV).

In our day when ear-splitting music threatens to, but never actually does, tear down walls, can we believe this? Will a gentle song, perhaps even the one written by the red-headed son of Jesse as he strummed on his harp and watched the quiet sheep, cause an earthquake?

Did Paul and Silas really sing Psalm 23?

It is possible. Today this Shepherd psalm is the best-known poem in the Scriptures. Would it have been less known then? Today it is the best-loved poem in the Scriptures. Would it have been less loved then? Today people in pain and problems recite Psalm 23. Would not they have done so then, also?

If the story of Paul and Silas and their earth-shaking midnight

6

concert is hard to believe, let me tell you another true story that took place only a few years ago:

This man knew he was going to die. Everything around him reminded him. Scratched crudely in the stone walls of the Singapore prison were the final words of many men before him who had faced death. Their curses, prayers, and occasionally their dreams were etched into the mildewed walls. Dampness gathered and fell like tears from the slimy stone.

Neivelle Tan did not weep. He did not pray. He did not hope. He only waited.

But for what? Not for pardon, for he had been condemned to die. He did not cry out against the charge, for there was no one to hear. The damp walls would echo his cry. He waited for lunch. That was all. A meager lunch of either noodles or rice and fish heads may not sound like a banquet to free men, but to men in solitary confinement, faced with death, it is something to look forward to.

The sound of sandals slapping against the concrete floor announced lunch time. In a moment, the brown plastic tray would be shoved through the slot in the steel door. He thought, Will there be extra noodles in the bowl? A bit more fish? Sometimes Neivelle was surprised by this luxury, and even more surprised by the thought that he had a friend on the outside. Some nameless person actually cared.

One day as the tray was slipped through the slot in the door it looked different. The bowl was the same, the scruffy brown tray was the same. A tiny wad of paper half hiding beside the bowl was the only difference.

Eagerly, Neivelle Tan reached for the paper, spread it out on the tray, and began to read the tiny page torn from a book—a Bible.

The Lord is my shepherd; I shall not want.
He maketh me to lie down in green pastures:
he leadeth me beside the still waters.
He restoreth my soul:
he leadeth me in the paths of righteousness
for his name's sake.
Yea, though I walk through the valley
of the shadow of death,
I will fear no evil:

7

for thou art with me;
thy rod and thy staff
they comfort me.
Thou preparest a table before me
in the presence of mine enemies:
thou anointest my head with oil.
my cup runneth over.
Surely goodness and mercy shall follow me
all the days of my life;
and I will dwell in the house of the Lord forever.

—Psalm 23

Can this be true? At least I know I have a friend somewhere in the prison, thought Neivelle. Perhaps, perhaps, I have a friend outside as well.

With little else to think about, with nothing else to read, he thought of these words from the ancient psalm—words he learned as a child. At the time he learned them, he had no idea that one day he would actually be in the "valley of the shadow of death."

How did I get here? he asked himself. Certainly not by asking the Lord to lead me. Like the other young people of my time, I thought that I was intelligent enough to make my own way, to make a pleasurable, maybe even a good life. But here in this slimy cell, I admit I have failed.

Finally Neivelle Tan, prisoner, condemned to death for murder, made the psalm his personal testimony. He asked the Lord to lead him. There was no hope of escape from the stone Singapore prison, but there was hope that even when death should come with the strangling hangman's noose, he would "dwell in the house of the Lord forever."

In the days that followed, the stone walls continued to be a prison for his body, but his spirit was set free. Free to dream, free to plan, free to pray.

Miraculously, one day he was taken from his death cell and allowed to mingle with the other prisoners. But Neivelle Tan was not content merely to mingle with them. He began to listen to them, talk with them, eventually to pray with them. Soon he was able to share the hope that he had found with other hopeless men.

At last he was pardoned. Set free. In the first pardon ever given by the governor of Singapore, the convict was set free. Prison walls had given way to the power of a song.

Today Neivelle Tan leads a congregation in the beautiful city of Singapore. He is a pastor—an undershepherd to the Great Shepherd. In a few weeks from the time I am writing these words, this man will be dedicating a lovely new building for his worshiping congregation. To people who are surrounded by enemies of all kinds, he will be spreading a table before them.

The story of Paul and Silas in a first-century Roman jail does not seem impossible to Neivelle Tan. Nor to me.

What amazing secret is contained in Psalm 23?

I am tempted to tell you another true story, a story that in its own way is even more remarkable than the two stories I have just told. Two reasons convince me that I should make you wait to hear this miraculous account. First I want to take a moment and talk about David's psalm. How does it relate to you? How can you make it more meaningful?

Second, I must wait to tell you the story that literally changed my whole idea of Scripture because at this stage in our discussion you are apt to be so shocked by it that you lay this book aside as a total fantasy.

Having said this, I realize that you can easily flip through the pages of this book and find the story, but when you read it, remember that I warned you. You really should wait. Even the most perfect shepherd, the Good Shepherd, cannot lead you a leap at a time, but a step at a time.

Chapter 3:

God's Amazing Secret

"If people would repeat Psalm 23 seven times before going to sleep each night, we would rarely see an emotional breakdown," said one thoughtful psychiatrist. Charles Allen, approaching it from the standpoint of a Bible scholar, simply calls this magnificent piece of poetry "God's psychiatry."

What magic lies in these 115 words? Their very familiarity may be their greatest handicap.

A legend from India talks of the time when the gods first made the earth. "Where shall we hide the secrets that will help people understand the word they live in?" they asked. "If they are too easily found, no one will discover them. Are the mountains high enough or are the oceans deep enough? Or are they too high or too deep?"

11

It was finally decided to hide these great truths in the most obvious places where people could see them all the time, but only the thoughtful would take time to look at them.

The legend has become a guide for my study of the Scriptures. Instead of probing into obscure passages that have puzzled scholars for years, I find that looking at those parts of the Bible that everyone thinks he or she already knows, is to discover God's most valuable secrets.

Very frankly, I asked the Lord to show me what was contained in the best known of all scriptures—the best known and often least understood, Psalm 23.

In my case, I had to overcome an emotional block. As a pastor I had so often been asked to read Psalm 23 at funeral services that I could almost smell flowers and see the tears on the faces of loved ones as I read it.

True, the psalm is a comfort when we walk through the valley of the shadow of death, but more important is God's leading us in the challenges of life.

With this thought in mind, I began a word-by-word—almost syllable-by-syllable—study of this ancient poem. In sharing them with others, I found the same amazement. Again and again, I found myself saying, "Does Psalm 23 really say this?"

Out of this study has come a series of lectures and now this book. My only authority will be the words of Scripture themselves. They will be my only commentary. As for the instructor, let us trust that the Good Shepherd himself will lead us to green pastures where our minds and our spirits can be nourished.

If this experience turns out to be amazing, so be it. Perhaps the most amazing secret of the entire experience will be that it took us so long to discover it.

Now that I have written this, I must confess that there will be an even greater surprise: the miracle that happens when the Lord truly becomes our shepherd. I have seen incredible changes in people as they explored Psalm 23. Sometimes the change is so dramatic that observant friends say, "What has happened to you? You are not the same person I knew a week ago."

Unfortunately, there doesn't seem to be a satisfactory answer for this kind of question. To say "I studied six verses of Scripture" only makes the questioner even more bewildered. Of course, there is the chance that the incredulous friend might be tempted to study the psalm himself or herself. No bad thing.

There is a reason for our reluctance to study Psalm 23 intensely. Getting into a "sheep" mentality is not easy for those of us who have been warned against "having the wool pulled over our eyes," or of being "sheepish."

For a shepherd boy on the rocky hillsides of Judea, it seemed perfectly natural to say, "The Lord is my shepherd." Just as the sharp-eyed lad watched the sheep and guarded them from the slinking wolves and prowling lions, God watched over Israel. And not just Israel as a nation, but each person.

For David it was a comforting thought.

For us, it would be comforting if we could believe it. But we find few shepherds listed in the yellow pages of our phone directories. Not many shoppers in the air-conditioned plazas of our cities would admit to looking for a shepherd.

But then, who in today's world wants to be a sheep?

A few months ago I watched three-year-old Jacob Lyon stand with his feet spread wide and a look of power on his face. "Who are you?" someone asked.

"I am Superman," he replied.

There is nothing sinister in this. He is merely a child of his times. What child in today's world is content to watch sheep nibbling on the stubbly grass and dream of being one. Today there are worlds to conquer, planets to attack, laser guns and silicon-chip marvels to fill the "want list."

Did I want to be Superman when I was a child? I try to remember. The earliest prayer I recall praying was a prayer taught to me by my Swedish parents: "I am a little, little lamb."

It is not likely that any parents are teaching that prayer to their children these days. Our culture makes it seem ridiculous. We simply do not want to be lambs. We don't want to bleat; we want to growl. We don't want to follow; we want to lead.

Courses on leadership are everywhere.

Recently I read of a man who had moved to a new community and talked to a pastor of a thriving church. "I would like to join your church, but I am afraid I am not much of a leader. I am more of a follower."

"Thank heavens, man. You are the one we are looking for. I have a whole congregation of would-be leaders who can't find anyone to follow them."

13

Again and again in this Psalm 23 we find God wanting to lead his people. Obviously God does not drive them with a whip; he simply leads them.

Experts with computerized data tell us that we can look into the future by analyzing the past. Experience is a good teacher, but a tardy one. It always teaches us the lesson we should have learned before we had the experience.

My friend, Holmes Brown, reminded me: "If we could sell our experience for what we paid for it, we would all be wealthy."

Indeed, who has not complained about the tuition in the school of experience?

Unfortunately, none of our lives will be lived in the past. All of our lives will be lived in the future. Who, then, can guide us into that future?

Only an eternal shepherd can see into the future.

To return to the poetic language of David's psalm, "The Lord is my shepherd." Surely the little woolly lambs learned that they did not need to study the geography of Judea in order to find the lunch line; they simply needed to keep their eyes on the shepherd. He would lead them. They did not need to worry about where he was leading them; they simply needed to assure themselves that he was leading them.

We could learn from their example. The Bible, fortunately, is not a book of philosophy to give us understanding about God. It is a book about obedience. Following the commands of God leads to a knowledge of God. It is the only way.

Obviously you have already invited the Lord to lead you or you would not have read this far. Why read further? Simply to explore the amazing things that God has promised to you if you will faithfully follow the Good Shepherd into the future.

The purpose of this book is to explore the ways of recognizing God's leadership, to examine the results of such an experience, and to tell the stories of people who have made the amazing discovery that God does indeed lead—today.

The Lord is my shepherd.
—Psalm 23:1

Chapter 4:

The *IS-NESS* of God

G etting God into the present tense is our first priority. Letting us know that he is in the present tense is God's first priority.

If God smiles (as I am sure he does) he must smile most often at our attempts to locate him in history and ignore him in the present day.

Personally I suspect that God is either amused or angered by our word *religion*. Religion, for the most part, is a person's attempt to warm himself by the ashes of yesterday's fire or to sail her boat by yesterday's wind.

Religions abounded in the day of Moses. He was schooled in all of them. But when God chose to show himself to Moses on the sandy plains of Midian, he made things very simple.

"Whom shall I say sent me?" Moses asked timidly.

"Say I AM sent you."

At this point Moses, already a little upset by a bush that persistently burned but just as stubbornly refused to be burned up, was reluctant to anger the Almighty. "Pardon me, I didn't quite get that" (free translation by Berquist).

"I AM that I AM."

God didn't waste words. God is a verb. An actor. A present reality.

You cannot find God in the history of the past. You can find the dusty footprints of God as he has worked in other times and in other places. This will assure you of the reality of God's presence in those times, but it will be little comfort for you if you need to know how to pay the rent on the thirtieth of the month.

Recently I talked with Les Sylvester in Canada. He told me of his very recent experience of asking God's help in his convenience-store business. "For years I believed in God, the Bible, and the traditional teachings of the church. But it never occurred to me that God could be available to help me in my business every day. It was not until I was totally discouraged, totally defeated, and totally hopeless that I learned that God is still around. Today.

"Now," said Les, "each morning when I rise I spend the first hour trying to discover how God wants me to run my business. It may sound crazy, but it's working. And you can't beat that."

You're right. You can't beat that.

What a tragedy that we do not understand that simple fact— God is.

The Hebrew faith has understood this about God. Nowhere can you find a statue or picture of God. It is not that the Hebrews were not artistic or skilled. It is simply that God does not stand still long enough for anyone to draw him. He moves so creatively that no one can predict his behavior.

Throughout the Scriptures, God speaks of himself in the present tense. Jesus declares himself: I am the bread of life. I am the way. I am the resurrection and the life. I am the good shepherd. Before Abraham was, I am.

Jesus refused to be imprisoned in the past. He still does.

We do not have to imagine Jesus' wearing a three-piece suit and carrying a leather attaché case with a JC monogram to make him at home in the twentieth century. Being all-wise, he understands

16

the now. And he will understand tomorrow.

We may outgrow the simplistic faith of our childhood, but we will never outgrow the eternal Lord. As Walter Horton said, he is "Our Eternal Contemporary."

To understand Psalm 23, we do not need to move to the country and sit on a rock while sheep graze peacefully around us. Oh, no, the Lord can lead us as we jet across the continent in order to be home in time for lunch. He still wants to lead us.

How desperately we need this. If we were wise enough to find our way by ourselves, how does it happen that so many of us are lost? And if we will not admit to being lost, we must surely confess that we have been bewildered for a terribly long time.

Convincing ourselves that God can be concerned about us individually may be the most difficult lesson we have to learn. It may indeed be the most important lesson that this wonderful psalm has to teach. Strange as it sounds, this simple truth needs to be retaught constantly.

Let me tell you how I learned a lesson only a few weeks ago.

I met God on Cherry Street in Seattle. Between Fourth Avenue and Fifth Avenue, I encountered the Almighty.

In my customary early-morning walk I was praying. Granted, it was a slightly desperate prayer because my well-made human plans had been blown apart by a sudden turn of events. I have more than I can carry, I thought. But, God, I am sure that you have more than you can carry, too. So I hate to bother you with my personal crisis.

Surrounded by the towering buildings of downtown Seattle, I felt that my personal crisis wasn't very big in comparison to the woes of a great city. Then I saw it. A tiny gray sparrow lay on the ground beside the lamp post. Obviously it had flown into the plate glass window of the Columbian Building, broken its neck, and had fallen lifeless to the earth.

"Are not two sparrows sold for a farthing," Jesus said. "Yet not one of them falls to the earth without your father. Are ye not of more value than many sparrows?"

Remembering this, I prayed once more. "Oh, Lord, you have time to notice the sparrow's fall, so I know you have time to lead me in the way I should go today."

Did I have to live more than half a century to learn this?

Apparently.

The Lord is my shepherd; I shall not want.

—Psalm 23:1

Chapter 5:

Me, Myself, and I— and God

When did self-consciousness become a sin? How can it be wrong for me to be aware of myself when God is aware of me? Certainly God does not sin. Nor do I when I think of myself.

Actually, there is nowhere else to start than with ourselves. Dean Inge, British writer of a few generations ago, said, "No man is obliged to be his own circumference, but he is obliged to be his own center."

Does this sound like selfishness? Is this heresy?

When I began a serious study of Psalm 23, I was well into it before a shattering thought came to me. This beautiful poem is bursting at the seams with the little pronoun *I*. Sometimes it is the possessive form *my,* and sometimes the objective form *me,* but it rears its spunky head again and again.

I began to underscore these words:

1. The Lord is MY shepherd;
2. I shall not want.
3. He maketh ME to lie down in green pastures:
4. he leadeth ME beside the still waters.
5. He restoreth MY soul:
6. he leadeth ME in the paths of righteousness for his name's sake.
7. Yea, though I walk through the valley of the shadow of death,
8. I will fear no evil:
9. For thou art with ME;
10. thy rod and thy staff they comfort ME.
11. Thou preparest a table before ME
12. in the presence of MINE enemies:
13. thou anointest MY head with oil;
14. MY cup runneth over.
15. Surely goodness and mercy shall follow ME
16. all the days of MY life:
17. and I will dwell in the house of the Lord forever.

Can we believe this? Seventeen times in six short verses the *I* occurs. Seventeen out of one hundred and fifteen words in the world's most beautiful poem are self-centered. *I* centered. What English teacher would have tolerated such a practice? What saint?

Yet this is a poem inspired by God.

Somewhere we have misunderstood. Feeling that we shouldn't be thinking of ourselves any time, we find ourselves thinking about ourselves all of the time. Being afraid to confront ourselves, we find that we are not able to avoid ourselves.

I one time watched a humble gray donkey. Tied by a long rope to a post, he tried to escape. Around and around he went, trying to stretch the rope to give himself a few more inches of freedom. But each time he wound himself closer and closer to the post. The more he tried to escape, the more captive he became.

We have the same problem. It is not a question of whether or not we want to deal with ourselves; we cannot escape ourselves.

20

Nor should we. Certainly we should not be ashamed of ourselves, since God is not.

Strangely, Jesus summarized all the Old Testament commands in two major commands. (1) Love the Lord your God with all your heart, with all your soul and with all your mind and (2) love your neighbor as yourself.

At first glance it appears that we ought immediately to turn from our worship of God to "loving other people." But we cannot avoid dealing with our own selfhood, our "I-ness." We can love others properly only as we properly love ourselves.

Caring people find it distasteful to give away a gift they feel to be worthless. Giving a gift on which you place no value is scarcely generosity. Nor is it love. The most precious gift God gave us is himself. And the most precious gift we give anyone is ourselves.

Gift wrapping ourselves may be our way to make every day Christmas.

Robert Schuller's book *Self Esteem—The New Reformation* seems almost a celebration of arrogance. David would have loved the book. In Psalm 23, he found no problem talking about himself—13.9% of the words in Psalm 23 are *I, me, mine, or my.*

It is impossible to bless God with one breath and curse human beings who are made in the likeness of God with the next breath. "Doth a fountain send forth at the same place both sweet water and bitter?" (James 3:11)

It is impossible to be "up" on God and "down" on yourself. You cannot truly love God unless you accept God's love for you.

The surest way to alienate people is to say bad things about their children. Even if the bad things are true, parents do not want to hear them. How do you think God feels if you ignore or criticize his children—particularly since you are one of them?

Is there a danger in this?

Of course there is. Recall Dean Inge's quote earlier that you are obliged to be your center, not your circumference. It is all right to begin with yourself in your experience with God, but it is deadly to end with yourself—to go no further than yourself.

In the Psalm of David, the Good Shepherd will lead you to a discovery of yourself and of the person you can become. But he will soon lead you to a life of service, a life of self-giving.

When you "gift wrap" yourself, the first person on your list is God. You give yourself away. When you claim "The Lord is my shepherd," you are also claiming to be God's sheep. You are giving away your independence, your life.

There are three awkward phrases that describe this process of being led by God:

*The *I*.
*The *IS*.
*The *HIS*.

Horrifying as this may be to English teachers, these three words comprise a sentence that summarizes all of Psalm 23: *I IS HIS*. Exploring the *I* is one of the most fascinating studies of life. What did God think of when he planned for your life? Did he put limits on your abilities? Did God dream for you what you are almost afraid to dream for yourself? Did he think of energy, health, vitality, joy, and blessing, or did God wish for you frustration, stress, sickness, poverty, and failure?

If you can imagine the sparkle in the eye of God when he thought about your birth, the joy he felt as he planned for your life, you will begin to understand how eager he is to lead you into the "green pastures" that will nourish your spirit. You will begin to understand his great love for you, his willingness to go out like a good shepherd and look for you when you have lost your way.

You may be down on yourself, but God is "up" on you. He cares. So we will talk about the *I* that appeared on God's drawing board as he planned for your life.

Then we will expand the *I* to an *IS*. We have talked about the *IS-ness* of you. Whatever your past has been, the present moment can be changed. Your future is not locked to your past, but to what happens in the present moment. You are a happening, a constantly changing bundle of possibilities.

Finally, and very importantly, we will discuss the third word of our cryptic sentence, *I IS HIS*. Starting with yourself, gift-wrapping yourself and realizing the value of yourself are important steps to fulfilled living. But they are all preparation for the one important step—giving yourself. Becoming *HIS*.

Of course, that is what the entire Psalm 23 is all about: caring enough about ourselves to want to follow the leadership of the one who created us, who loved us, and who gave himself for us. Learning how to recognize God's leadership and being willing to follow it are two of life's most important skills.

Progressing from the *I-ness* to the *IS-ness* to the *HIS-ness* is a lifetime project. And, since it is going to take so long to complete the journey, we really ought to begin it immediately.

Psalm 23 is a wonderful map, but a map is not the journey. The six short verses of Psalm 23 can be repeated in thirty-three seconds, but they may never be fully understood. I personally have spent at least forty years studying these 115 words and I have spoken and written thousands of words about them, but each day that I invite the Good Shepherd to lead me, I am learning more and more about them.

This may be the reason I have waited so long to write this book: I never seem to be ready. So I invite you to study Psalm 23, live by it, and write a book about your experience.

I will look forward to reading it.

Chapter 6:

How Does It Work in Real Life?

The ringing phone startled me. Realizing that I was the only one in the house, I decided to answer it.

"Are you the preacher?" a stranger asked.

"Well, I am not the pastor of the church, but I am a preacher. Can I help you?"

"Do you pray for people?"

"Yes."

"We need someone right away. Mama is sick and we don't know what to do. Can you come?"

"Of course. Tell me how to get to your house."

In minutes I was standing on the weatherbeaten front porch of a modest home in Ohio. I knocked and waited.

Even before anyone answered my knock, I heard pitiful screams coming from inside the house. They reminded me of the bleating of an animal caught in a steel trap.

Soon a pale-faced teen-ager came to let me in. "Mama is real sick, and we don't know what to do. We're scared. She is acting crazy."

I was led to a bedroom and as we approached, the screaming became louder. No voice could be heard above it. The anguished voice of a woman in pain pierced the air. "Can't you see? They are trying to kill me. Help me. Help me."

What could I do?

"Let's pray," I said. Bowing my head, closing my eyes, and trying to shut out the stabbing cries, I prayed silently that the Lord would teach me how to pray for this woman.

In a moment I began to pray out loud. Without knowing why, I began repeating Psalm 23, the Shepherd's Psalm:

> The Lord is my shepherd,
> I shall not want.
> He maketh me to lie down in green pastures:
> he leadeth me beside the still waters.
> He restoreth my soul:
> he leadeth me in the paths of righteousness
> for his name's sake.
> Yea, though I walk through the valley
> of the shadow of death,
> I will fear no evil:
> for thou art with me;
> thy rod and thy staff they comfort me.
> Thou preparest a table before me
> in the presence of mine enemies:
> thou anointest my head with oil;
> my cup runneth over.
> Surely goodness and mercy
> shall follow me all the days of my life:
> and I will dwell in the house of the Lord forever.

When I finished this prayer the air seemed somewhat quieter. The familiar words "The Lord is my shepherd" seemed a million miles away from this room of anguish and pain. The "still waters"

26

of the shepherd seemed a world away from the turbulence of a woman tossing about on the bed.

I began a second time.

Then a third time. As I began quietly repeating the words of this psalm, I heard a voice join mine. The sick woman was speaking. At first there was only a phrase or a sentence. By the time we repeated the psalm the fourth time, she was saying it perfectly. Stored somewhere in her troubled mind was this treasure of Scripture. Perhaps she had learned it as a child when her only reason for learning it was to get a gold star pasted on a piece of paper.

Now, in the hour of her desperate need, Psalm 23 had come to life. It reached her in a place her conscious mind could not reach. No one else could "impose this truth on her." The answer had to come from within.

As we finished repeating Psalm 23, I said reverently, "Amen." When I opened my eyes, I saw this terrified woman lying peacefully on the bed, smiling a quizzical smile. "Who are you, and where did you come from?" she asked.

"I am a preacher and I have come to pray for you. You have been very sick and the Lord has healed you."

"I can't remember. I can't remember. I feel like I have been on a long journey, but I don't know where I have been." The plain and simple fact is that God had miraculously and instantaneously healed her. I hope she will never remember the agonizing hours that brought me to her house, but I will never forget. The phrase "the valley of the shadow of death" has a special meaning for me as I repeat David's psalm.

As I drove home my mind buzzed with a thousand questions. What had happened? How had it happened? Can it happen again? Is there a magic power in these 115 words of Psalm 23, or is it a power that lives in Scripture when we take time to plant it in our subconscious mind? What did David mean when he said, "Thy word have I hid in my heart that I might not sin against thee?" (Psalm 119:11).

Obviously there is more to "hiding God's Word" in our hearts than merely reading it or even memorizing it. There is more to believing God's Word than simply compiling lists of Scripture verses under alphabetical headings.

All of these thoughts and many others made me decide to do

two things. First, I would analyze Psalm 23 as intensely as I could and second, I would try to plant its teachings in my own mind and in the mind of others so that when a desperate need arises, I will have resources on hand to meet the need.

In the years that have passed, I have witnessed many miracles very much like the one that took place at the beginning of my ministry. Although my faith is stronger than ever, I am still amazed by what happens.

This book is intended as a do-it-yourself manual for those who really want to explore the possibilities of being led by a good shepherd whose dreams for us are more wonderful than our own.

Chapter 7:

I Am Free
to Choose Bondage

At first glance, Psalm 23 seems to be a self-centered psalm, what with seventeen *I* words in the six short verses. That is why it pays to examine it again carefully.

When we say, "The Lord is my shepherd," the choice is ours, but it is really the last choice we get to make or the last choice we want to make. For, claiming the Lord as our shepherd means that we have given ourselves away—our rights, our will, and our plans.

Claiming the Lord as shepherd does not mean that we possess God, but that God possesses us.

Without question, most people have a god of some sort. It is scarcely civilized, not to mention cultured, to be without a deity of some description. The tragedy is that people make gods that they can manipulate and control. For such a divinity-on-a-string to try to control their lives would be unthinkable.

In this way, they may possess a God, but their god in no way possesses them. Such a god serves their purpose very well as long as they do not have any very great purpose or any desperate need. Unfortunately, if a man should be lost, it is doubtful that the little wind-up god he has in his pocket could save him.

Less ambitious people than the god-makers timidly accept the gods and goals of others. Their lives fall into the ruts that others have worn for them. If these ruts are sufficiently sanctimonious, they are called religion.

But a personal shepherd, who can believe it?

The moment we say "The Lord is my shepherd" we feel faintly selfish, or even decidedly stupid. "How," we ask, "can God give full time to me as well as every other person in the world?"

Recently, veteran missionary Ann Smith told of a woman in Japan who became a Christian. She knew that she needed to pray, but she felt self-conscious about bothering the Almighty. So, in order to avoid overburdening God, she would stay awake until one o'clock in the morning to pray because she felt that he wouldn't be so busy at that time.

We smile at her simplicity, knowing that one o'clock in Tokyo is noon somewhere else in the world. But still we need to be reminded that not being a prisoner in time, God can take time for each of us.

One day in a lecture, I said, "One thing we know: God loves people."

Albert Donaldson, creative and perceptive friend, met me later. "You made a mistake, Berquist. God does not love people."

I couldn't believe he was serious. But he was. "God does not love people. He loves persons, individuals."

I have to agree. And Al's distinction is important. It is also scriptural.

In another of his psalms, David says:

How precious are thy thoughts unto me, O God.
how great is the sum of them!
If I should count them,
They are more in number than the sand:
when I awake, I am still with thee.
—Psalm 139:17, 18

30

God is thinking about you right now. Not only is God aware of the person you know that you are, but God is also aware of the person he knows you can become. God is tremendously eager to lead you, but he will not insist on it. The Lord may indeed be the Great Shepherd, the Good Shepherd; this is his nature. But he will not be your shepherd until you sincerely ask him to be.

Is this bondage? Yes, it is, but look for a moment at what your freedom to choose your own way has brought you. Oscar Wilde made us think with these words:

> In this world, there are only two tragedies. One is not getting what one wants, and the other is getting it.

The frustration and failure of self-will certainly are not to be compared with the fulfillment of life when the Lord leads. But the choice is ours.

The Lord is my shepherd; I shall not want.

—Psalm 23:1

Chapter 8:

What Is Lacking?

What if everyone got everything he or she wanted when he or she wanted it? What if it never rained on anyone's parade? What if our slightest wish was God's command?

The prospect is frightening. If it never rained on anyone's picnic, it would never rain on anyone's parsnips or petunias either, because someone is surely having a picnic every day of the week.

Who could live in such a world? Or who would want to? Does this verse of Psalm 23 mean that, like sheep, we are going to be cared for so thoroughly that we need never think about anything except our overweight problem? If that were true, we would live lives of such undisciplined and upholstered comfort that we would die of boredom.

Another possible interpretation of this verse is that God would respond to every childish request we made.

Watch a small boy being taken through a toy store by his grandmother. (Children quickly learn that grandparents are the best kind of escort for such a trip.)

"I want one of these," the lad says, picking up toy after toy.

"If you really want it, I'll get it for you." Grandparents are like that.

When the boy and his grandmother leave the store, they carry a large bundle of the "wanted" toys. Once home, the boy abandons the toys in a pile and proceeds to amuse himself with something else.

"I thought you wanted all these things," the grandparent says.

"But grandmother, I don't always want all the things I want," he replies.

If we smile at this, we must smile guardedly. A Saturday-morning drive through almost any American city will reveal a strange sight—the garage sale. Displayed on driveways, porches, and in garages are mountains of gadgets people thought they couldn't live without. Now they can't live with them.

Despair not. Someone wants them. With the money we retrieve from these trinkets, we can fill the garage again with more things we want. How many family budgets are trampled to death by these white elephants!

To understand what David meant by saying "I shall not want," we need to look at the scriptural use of the word *want*.

Psalm 34 gives us a clue:

> O taste and see that the Lord is good:
> blessed is the man that trusteth in him.
> O fear the Lord, ye his saints:
> for there is no want to them that fear him.
> The young lions do lack, and suffer hunger:
> but they that seek the Lord
> shall not want any good thing.
> —Psalm 34:8-10

In these verses, we see both the word *want* and the word *lack* used to describe not casual desires or fleeting wishes, but fundamental needs.

Another illustration of this comes from the story of Belshazzar, the Babylonian king.

A lavish feast was planned for the king and thousands of his lords. Everything money could buy or power could command was made available to the king and his guests. Even the most degrading human desires were indulged. A drunken orgy, a sexual debauch, followed.

In the midst of this lavish orgy, the fingers of a man's hand appeared and began to write on the plaster of the wall. Among the strange words that appeared was TEKEL. Not knowing what the word meant, the king asked his wise men. They didn't know, either.

To a Hebrew lad Daniel, God gave the interpretation of this cryptic message: "This is the meaning: You are weighed in the balances and found wanting."

Certainly God did not mean by his use of the word *wanting* that Belshazzar was too poor to provide for the party. Nothing was off-limits to the king. Even the sacred golden vessels stolen from the temple in Jerusalem were used as wine flagons. Every base desire of drunken men and women was indulged without question.

But in the scales of God's righteousness, the king was lacking—lacking and desperately needy.

Many times in the New Testament, we are assured of God's willingness to provide for our needs. No verse is more forceful than the words of the Apostle Paul:

> But my God shall supply all your need according to his riches in glory by Christ Jesus.
> —Philippians 4:19

A sign painted on the wall of a Caribbean mission said simply:

> Where God guides,
> God provides.

In another place I saw a motto:

> God is willing to take complete responsibility for any life committed to his leadership.

35

When I find myself in some bleak wasteland of despair and discouragement, I have learned to ask myself, Who led you to this place? When I get honest enough to answer my question, I find the words of James helpful:

> Ye ask, and receive not,
> because ye ask amiss,
> that ye may consume it
> upon your lusts.
> —James 4:3

What a jolting thought! God's provision, protection, and promises are for those who follow his guidance. For those who fail to follow, there is frustration, futility, and failure.

What is even more surprising, God is willing to supply not only what we need for survival, but also with whatever we need to fulfill his dreams for our future. Frankly, we don't even know what we lack, because we don't know what we could be.

So to start with, we lack an understanding of what we lack. But fear not. God will supply that need as well—if we follow.

Chapter 9:

God's Possibility Book

Generally speaking, we do not ask for directions unless we know we are lost. We do not ask God to lead us if we are satisfied with things as they are now. As a result, modern people do not find the gospel impossible; they simply find it unnecessary. With no higher goal than survival, they feel perfectly competent to direct their own lives.

When the noted psychiatrist Karl Menninger wrote his fascinating book *Whatever Became of Sin?* he startled us all into thinking. Obviously, sin is still around, but the painful awareness of it is missing. Why?

Every serious student of the Scriptures knows that the most commonly used Greek word for *sin* means "missing the mark."

But if we have no idea what the mark is, how will we know if we have missed it? If we do not know that we are lost, how will we look for a shepherd? Even if the shepherd is looking for us, will we welcome him when he finds us?

For the most part we are godless, not because we cannot believe in a supreme being, but because we are satisfied to find our own way in the world. We are, as T.S. Eliot describes us:

> The decent godless people,
> whose only monument is the asphalt road
> and a thousand lost golf balls.

Such people blend with the world around them and "set their watches by the public clocks." The protective coloration of the majority of their peers seems to insulate them from their divine possibilities. So they live and die without ever having really lived.

To be told they are lost would be unthinkable. Like sheep, scrawny from nibbling on barren hillsides, their spiritual malnutrition is apparent to everyone but themselves. Our only hope for them is that they will one day hear a voice that calls them on to better things—the voice of the Good Shepherd.

When that happens, will they—or more correctly—will we hear it? It is possible we will not. Why not?

For starters, our fascination with superficiality distracts us.

I think of a gift I brought back to America from Japan. This was years ago, and I was a young student with little money to spend. But as I traveled, I bought gifts that I thought my friends might enjoy.

In Tokyo, I saw a pretty set of salt and pepper shakers. Gracefully designed of sterling silver, they were shaped like tiny pagodas. I bought them.

Returning to America, I tried to think of someone who would enjoy them. Eunice Morrison, wife of our college president, came to mind. She was one of the most gracious hostesses I knew. Often I had been invited to share a meal or a snack in her home. She would enjoy the silver salt and pepper shakers. I could scarcely wait to present them to her.

Mrs. Morrison was not only a gracious hostess, she was a genuinely grateful person. Even before unwrapping my gift, she expressed her delight.

"Why don't you unwrap it," I suggested.

She unfastened the wrapping and discovered the wooden box that contained the set. Her gratitude exploded into new words of thankfulness.

"Oh, what a beautiful box. Thank you so much for it. I am flattered to think that you would remember me while you were away. I am sure I will find many uses for this box, and I will always remember that you gave it to me."

On and on she went, a veritable fountain of gratitude.

Frankly, I could not blame her for being impressed with the carefully crafted wooden box, but I was embarrassed by her effusive thanks. The box was not the gift. But I had to wait until her avalanche of thanks stopped. Then I said, "Why don't you look inside the box? That's where the present is."

As I remember the incident, I can see the momentary expression of frustration that flashed across her face. She was virtually speechless as she lifted the exquisite silver pieces out of the box. She had used all her superlatives on the box and had none left for the contents.

I am sure God is pleased with our gratitude for life and breath, for food and shelter. But life is more than this. His goals for us are more than substance.

God wants to supply not only what we need to live, but what we need to live up to.

If we were to make a list of all the things we want from God, I doubt that it would be as long as the list of things that God wants to give to us. If we stretch our imaginations to the limit to dream of all that we would like to become, it is doubtful that we could dream as much for ourselves as God has dreamed for us.

Next, satisfaction with mediocrity.

Unless the sheep believes that the shepherd knows of greener pastures than the ones on which it is now feeding, will it willingly follow the shepherd? If we, as the sheep of God's pasture, do not expect much out of life, will we eagerly seek his leadership to more exciting ventures? How will we ask God to lead if we do not know what we lack?

The prophet Isaiah understood how difficult it is for us to "unwrap" the package ourselves:

For since the beginning of the world

men have not heard, nor perceived by the ear,
Neither hath the eye seen, O God,
beside thee, what he hath prepared for him
that waiteth for him.

—Isaiah 64:4

The Apostle Paul echoed this idea when he wrote:

Eye hath not seen, nor ear heard,
neither have entered into the heart of man,
the things which God hath prepared
for them that love him.

—1 Corinthians 2:9

Paul does not stop there. Nor should we. He continued:

But God hath revealed them unto us by his Spirit
for the spirit searcheth all things,
yea, the deep things of God. . . .
Now we have received, not the spirit of the world,
But the spirit which is of God;
That we might know the things
That are freely given to us of God.

—1 Corinthians 2:10, 12

As we venture further into a study of Psalm 23, we will discover many ways that the Lord can lead us. We will also recognize some of the places where we can easily miss the path.

These are important lessons.

But no lesson is more important than learning to trust God's vision of our future rather than our own. At this point, I must tell you a story about the early years of my married life.

Although I was thirty before I married, I did not understand some basic facts of life. For one thing, I certainly did not know how women think.

While I make no claim of explaining the feminine mind in this book, I will attempt to explain at least one part of one female's mind.

Many women do not like to shop, but my wife's fondness for it will help bring up the national average. Let me tell you how I discovered this fact of life.

One day I asked my beautiful young bride what she would like to do, and she replied that she would like to go shopping.

"For what?" I asked naively.

"How do I know until I see what they've got?"

I must express my thanks to my wife for helping me to understand the basic need of believers—the need to know the possibilities.

How do we know what we lack until we see what God has provided for us?

Several different people have been credited with the following quotation, so you are free to choose whichever one suits your political position and opinion:

Some people look at things as they are and say, "Why?"
I look at things as they can be and say, "Why not?"

One of the most exciting journeys any of us could take would be a shopping trip in the supermarket of God's dreams for us. If for one moment we could see what we can be, we would be dissatisfied with anything less. Such a journey into the world of possibilities cannot be taken with your eyes. Nor with your ears. You must take it with your heart. God's spirit will lead you. You do not need to want.

Thou preparest a table before me in the presence of mine enemies.
—Psalm 23:5

Chapter 10:

When You Get to Tomorrow, God Has Already Been There

Everything begins with a plan. The wiser the planner, the better the plan.

Have you heard the statement, "You ought to plan for your future, because you are going to spend the rest of your life there?" This sounds like good advice. Even better advice would be to trust your life to the eternal God, because you are going to spend eternity somewhere. God has planned ahead. So should you.

One day in Michigan I stood in a bookstore autographing copies of my book *The Doctor Is In.* From across the store a woman came running.

"I want to buy this book," she said. "There is one statement in it that is worth the entire price."

The customer opened the book and began to read, "You are not an accident of either your parents or nature. You are a prized creation of the greatest Creator, God."

"All my life," she said, "my parents have told me that I was an unwanted child. Whenever I displeased them they would say, 'Well, you know we didn't really plan for you or want you.' As a result, I have spent twenty-seven years feeling worthless. Just now, reading your book, I realized that God had plans for me, even if my parents didn't. I feel I am worth something."

Most of us don't have to struggle with that kind of cruel rejection, but our secular society encourages us to believe that we are an unplanned event in the universe. An unwanted child. Even devout believers sometimes give little thought to the preparations God has made for our future.

When David wrote, "Thou preparest a table before me in the presence of mine enemies," he was not thinking of a twentieth-century housekeeper putting gleaming china and crystal on a linen tablecloth (possibly with a critical mother-in-law looking on.) The "table" he had in mind was different. The preparation was different.

During the winter months in Judea, the sheep were pastured in the lowlands. When the snows began to melt on the mountains, knowing spring was on its way, the shepherd left the flock in the care of an undershepherd and went to the mountains. There he planned for the summer pastures. Finding a flat area where grasses grew, he prepared it for his flocks. Because land that grows tender grass also can grow poisonous weeds, he carefully pulled out all the harmful weeds.

His preparation was twofold: first he marked the path to the new pastures, making sure he had found a path that the sheep could follow. Then he took away anything that could hurt them. Such work was lonely work, and only the shepherd realized how important it was.

As we think of ourselves as "sheep of his pasture" we can find comfort in the preparations that God has made for our future. If the path to new pastures seems a little rocky, we ought to realize that our shepherd thinks the journey is worth it.

Who were the enemies that can keep us from beginning such a journey? In David's time, they were lions, bears, and wolves. Today these animals are rarely found in Israel, even in zoos, but there are emotional and spiritual enemies in the world in which we

44

all live. Our greatest danger is that they don't look like enemies. Sometimes they are wolves in three-piece wool suits, wolves in sheep's clothing, to be sure, but very stylish and very processed sheep's clothing.

Who are these enemies, these rogues that threaten our spiritual journey?

1. FAMILY AND FRIENDS

Why is it that those who say they want the best for us keep us from becoming our best? Why indeed did Jesus say, "A man's foes shall be they of his own household?" (Matthew 10:36).

Often we are imprisoned in the low expectations of our fathers and mothers, not to mention competitive brothers and sisters! Even Jesus found it difficult to do many mighty works in his hometown of Nazareth. "Is not this the carpenter's son? is not his mother called Mary? and his brethren, James, and Joses, and Simon, and Judas? And his sisters, are they not all with us? Whence then hath this man all these things? (Matthew 13:55-56).

Parental love can become smother love. The very fact that our families accept us as we are and really would love to keep us that way means that they will resent our dreams of better things.

Sometimes this unbelief turns to ridicule, sometimes even to hate. The Bible story of Joseph reminds us.

Joseph was the favorite of his father's twelve children. His older brothers put him down. In a dream Joseph saw a sheaf of wheat in a field to which all the other sheaves were bowing. He dreamed again and this time the sun, moon, and stars were bowing down to him (Genesis 37:7-9).

Little wonder his brothers hated him when he told them his dreams. Fortunately, Joseph refused to be bound to family expectations. He remembered his dreams.

The path through which God led Joseph to the fulfillment of his dreams was a long and difficult one. He was sold into slavery, accosted by Potipher's wife, and betrayed by friends. But still he remembered his youthful dreams. In due time, Joseph became a ruler in Egypt and lived to see his brothers bow down to him. The time even came when they were proud of him.

Your family and friends are important. They helped start your career; don't let them finish it.

2. CONFORMITY

Simply because the Bible tells us that we are sheep does not mean that we should move in flocks. God leads us individually. When Paul the apostle tells us to "be not conformed to this world" (Romans 12:2) he might well have added, "and do not be conformed to the other members of the church." Conformity is deadly.

In the New Testament, we are told that Jesus "called his sheep by name." Each is different. Our responsibility is to follow the shepherd and not the other sheep.

A wise observer said, "There is no known formula for success, but there is one for failure: try to please everybody."

The easiest way to distinguish between human-made religions and God's salvation is at the point of conformity. Religions press people into their molds; God helps people to break out of the molds. Emerson said, "To be great is to be misunderstood." Risk it.

3. DESIRE FOR ACCEPTANCE

Young people have an intense desire for acceptance. In fact, they will often pay almost any price to be part of the crowd. As the years pass, this intensity somewhat lessens, but all of us want to be accepted.

That being true, logic would dictate doing whatever most people do, so that we will be accepted by the greatest number of people. Democracy seems to suggest that the majority is right.

A school teacher invited her young students to bring their pets to school for Show and Tell. One child brought a rabbit.

"Is it a boy rabbit or a girl rabbit?" the children asked.

"I don't know," said the teacher. "Let's vote on it." This first-grade vote may have been a lesson in democracy, but it was scarcely a lesson in biology. Or reality.

Collecting the opinions of friends may seem to give us some sense of security in choosing our life path, but it may mean that we throw away our eternal opportunity. "Thou shalt not follow a multitude to do evil," says the Scripture (Exodus 23:2).

Even when obedience to God's plan means loneliness, it is far better to be separated from a few sheep than to be separated from the shepherd.

4. PAGAN SENSUALITY

"If it feels good, do it," says the modern hedonist. "Obey every urging of your body and mind and you will live a fulfilled life. This is nature's way," they continue.

46

Of course it doesn't work that way.

Sheep do not find green pastures by wandering off to explore the most succulent grasses. This is how they get lost and become prey for the wolves. Leaderless sheep are defenseless.

So are we.

As an exercise in obedience, I strongly recommend fasting—going without food for a time. To be sure, there are physical benefits from this, but they are secondary. The first thing you will discover when you decide to miss a specified number of meals for the sake of a spiritual goal is that your physical appetite is stronger than you thought. Fasting doesn't feel good. Not at first—in fact, not for quite a while. But being able to prove to yourself that you have stronger motivations than physical appetite is worth the effort.

5. THE PRISON OF STATISTICS

If you are content to be average, you certainly won't be superior. Strangely, you won't even be normal. If you measure yourself by what others accept as being right for them, you cannot achieve what God has planned for you.

Evangelist Ewald Wolfram reminds us that the "average" person has only 1.9 legs.

He reaches this conclusion by counting all the legs in the country and then dividing that figure by the number of people. Obviously some people are born without two legs, some have lost one or both legs, either in an accident or through surgery. So the average is 1.9.

With only 1.9 legs, you will limp.

Statistics can be a prison to limit the achievers and to comfort the losers. In both cases, they are an enemy.

6. HIRELINGS

Jesus recognized some shepherds as "hirelings," and so we may call them by the same name. The hireling does not care for the sheep, but only what they can do for him. He is the manipulator.

In an earlier book *When You Feel Like a Misfit* I talked about the "cookie-cutter mentality." People who think this way will flatten you out, roll over you, and cut you into whatever shape they need or want to use.

Like a baker making gingerbread men, they have their cookie cutters all ready as soon as they find someone who will submit to their plans. If they need someone to absorb their guilt, they will lay it on you. If they need someone to dominate in order to feel important, they will dominate you. If they need someone to lean on, they will lean on you so that they can blame you if they fall.

If you submit to these hirelings, you will be led to your death. And what is worse, you will have died for an unworthy cause. You did not even give your life for "another sheep." You do not strengthen others by giving in to their weakness.

Parents, employers, brothers, and sisters (both in the church and in the family) will be glad to lay their "cookie cutter" on you. This is not good for you. Nor is it good for them.

7. UNDUE RESPECT FOR OTHERS' OPINIONS

I am not what I think I am.
I am not what you think I am.
But I am what I think you think I am.

So goes an old quotation about who we are. We all tend to fall into the pattern of what others expect us to be. And that is wrong. Sometimes people expect too much and sometimes they expect too little.

8. THE PRISON OF THE PAST

If you live in the brown barren hills of memory, you will not find the green pastures. You can't live on yesterday's guidance. You cannot be nourished forever on the success of the past. And even more important, you need not be imprisoned by yesterday's failures.

It is not bad to be sick. You can recover from sickness. To be "sickly" is a sentence of death. It is the acceptance of the pain of the past as a prophecy of the future.

You are not a failure merely because you have failed. Your future is not scarred merely because your childhood or your marriage was unsuccessful or painful. The Lord will lead you out of your past—unless you insist on carrying your past with you.

To return to Psalm 23, the sheep under David's care did not forget that their shepherd had successfully dealt with their enemies. They had seen him kill a lion and had seen him hurl a stone with deadly accuracy at a slinking wolf. As they nibbled on the green grass to which he had led them, they felt no fear. He had spread a table before them in the presence of their enemies.

In our day, spiritual stupidity would say we have no enemies.

Mature trust says, We have enemies, but our shepherd can over-come them.

The Lord is . . . —Psalm 23:1

Chapter 11:

The *IS-NESS* of Psalm 23

In the preceding chapter, we talked about the prison of the past. It is filled with the skeletons of abandoned dreams and broken promises. The good news is that you do not need to live in that gloomy place. You are not a "was," but an "is." Whatever you were yesterday, you do not need to be today. Even more amazing, whatever you are at this moment, you do not need to be five minutes from now.

As we study Psalm 23, we discover to our surprise that the personal pronoun *I* is used seventeen times in its various forms, such as me, mine, and my. Of the 115 words of this poem 13.9 percent are *I*-centered.

Now we must acknowledge an even more important idea: the *I* is an *IS*. In fact, the Lord himself is an *IS*. "The Lord IS my shepherd," David says. Through the psalm, eight other verbs are used to describe the word of this good shepherd—and every single one of them is in the present tense!

Releasing God from the prison of the past may be the first thing some of us have to do! We must keep reminding ourselves that what God said to Moses, he is still saying to us: "I am." God is a verb.

Even more important for our discussion is that you are a verb. You are a constantly changing accumulation of energy.

In the same way that the sheep in David's song are led to pastures, water, and fulfillment, you are being led to a wonderful life—the life God planned for you before the world itself existed. You are being led, that is, if you are willing to release the past and not worry about the future.

You will not find this fulfillment on your own. "There is a way that seemeth right unto a man," says Proverbs, "but the end thereof are the ways of death" (14:12). So you can't trust yourself. But you can trust the Lord.

To enter the fascinating world of your present possibilities, we will first of all talk about your physical body.

Every school child knows that we are composed of atoms that in turn are composed of electrons. It is not important for us to understand all that scientists know about these tiny building blocks of all matter, but we must think about them simply, as school children are taught to think about them.

To get an idea of their size, let us look at a grain of sand. If we were to magnify the grain of sand until it was as large as a hundred story building, the atom within it would be the size of the head of a pin.

Then if we were to magnify that pinhead until it was as large as a football field, the electron within it would be the size of a fly on the fifty-yard line. Everything else within the grain of sand is space.

Of course, the atoms are moving around in this world of space as are the electrons within the atom. The number of these energetic particles within a substance determines its density. A very dense material might be metal, while a less dense one might be wood. Even less dense ones would be gas.

If we could visualize this, we could quickly see two things, space and movement.

In the words of a theoretical physicist, "Matter is simply the way energy behaves."

What does this mean to us who are trying to understand ourselves? It simply means that we are constantly becoming something. We are not chained to the past, whatever it is. We are either becoming better or worse.

If the Good Shepherd is leading us, we are becoming better. He restores our soul. He nourishes our dreams and our life. We are not only fulfilled, but we are filled to overflowing; our cup "runneth over."

It is sad that religion as it is popularly conceived is so much taken up with form rather than force. The Apostle Paul speaks of those who "have a form of godliness, but deny the power thereof." Could he be speaking of us?

I'd like you to meet Sarah. I have changed her name for this story, but the facts are just as I relate them.

The mother of nine children, Sarah came to the lectures I was giving on Psalm 23. The droop of her shoulders and the drawn expression on her face made me wonder if the pilot light in her soul had gone out. I found myself watching her as I explained and talked about the amazing secrets in Psalm 23. Occasionally I would notice a flash of inspiration as an idea seemed to strike her with particular force. As the days passed, these flashes of inspiration seemed to come more frequently. The change was remarkable. She began to immerse herself in the song of David. Her spirit began to be nourished in the green pastures into which the Lord himself was leading her. Her soul was restored.

By the time the week was ending, people on the convention grounds began stopping her to ask, "What has happened to you? I have known you for years, but I can scarcely recognize you as the same person."

Whatever Sarah had been, she was no longer. It was as though a butterfly had emerged from what had been a crawling worm. Is such a thing possible? Indeed it is—not only for Sarah, but for anyone who will sincerely ask the Lord to become her or his shepherd.

A few weeks ago, I read a statement from Jim Smoke, counselor to people who are trying to rebuild their lives after a traumatic divorce:

Sure you can fly again,
But that cocoon has got to go.

The cocoon of which he speaks is the hard-fixed idea of what we have been—the prison of the past. God is certainly willing to lead us into the future, but we cannot take our past along with us. For we are not a "was" but an "is."

He maketh me to lie down in green pastures.

—Psalm 23:2

Chapter 12:

Nourishing the New You

What pictures these words paint: emerald green pastures, cool, clear pools of water. In such a paradise sheep could not help being healthy and happy.

People, too, should be happy in such a place. In a world of ringing telephones, screeching tires, and threatening deadlines, green pastures seem like a fantasy.

When I first read Psalm 23, I was a child in Kansas. In those days Kansas was the center of the dust bowl. Relentless sun baked the dry earth until it cracked open. The promise of rain taunted farmers with the possibility that some day the fields would be green again.

It was not to be. Instead of rain, the sun burned down and the cracks in the brick-hard earth became wide enough to step into. Cattle died unless their owners could haul water from distant springs.

Surrounded by this kind of drought, I often thought of the verdant fields in David's psalm. In my mind I could visualize these lush pastures—fields of clover so luxuriant that the sheep could wander around and be scarcely visible.

This is the picture I carried in my mind as I thought of Israel, the land of the Bible.

What a surprise waited for me when I actually arrived in Israel for the first time. Israel is a land of rock.

Shepherds in Israel have a saying: "A goat could walk from Dan in the north to Beersheba in the south simply by stepping from stone to stone."

There is even a legend that explains Israel's rocky terrain. Once upon a time when God was first creating the earth, he decided that every land ought to have a few stones. So he sent an angel with a large bag of stone to fly over the earth and instructed him to give a fair share to each part of the earth. According to the legend, when the angel flew over Israel, the bag broke. The story is easy to believe. In Israel, stone fences are everywhere. Something has to be done with the rocks to allow a little ground to be used for growing things.

Where, then, are the green pastures of which David sings?

Is Psalm 23 only poetry, or is it a fact?

Indeed green pastures still exist in Israel today as in David's time. Sheltered by the towering mountains are meadows lush with grass. Rushing down the mountainsides are clear streams that can become pools of crystal waters. But they cannot be seen from the dusty road. Only the shepherd knows where they are.

If sheep could find them by themselves, there would be no need of a shepherd. They might easily graze on the open lands like wild beasts.

Not only this, but without the shepherd there might be no pastures. For not only does he find the pastures, he nurtures them. Pastures, you see, need care as well as sheep.

Without the watchful eye of a diligent shepherd, the fields would soon be trodden down by the sheep. Poisonous weeds would spring up. Parasites and vermin would flourish.

A careful shepherd not only finds new pastures, but he keeps looking for newer ones so that the older ones can have a chance to renew themselves.

David's observation "He maketh me to lie down in green pastures" becomes significant when we are told that sheep, grazing where the grass is abundant, lie down and rest. In this way the nourishment has a chance to build their bodies. It is not uncommon for sheep in such pastures to gain a hundred pounds in as many days.

On the other hand, if the grass is sparse and dry, the sheep move continually about, grubbing at roots and dry vegetation trying to satisfy their hunger. They lose weight. They are not satisfied.

How beautifully this illustrates God's care for us, the sheep of his pasture. The psalmist echoes this idea in Psalm 103: "[The Lord] satisfieth thy mouth with good things so that thy youth is renewed like the eagle's" (Psalm 103:5).

In our day, gaunt spiritual pilgrims who seem never to be satisfied are a common sight. From book to book, conference to conference, they journey, becoming more frustrated daily. Intense they are. But happy, no. Even to appear happy would seem frivolous.

Such restless sheep are easy victims of the newest and most bizarre cults. They are, as Paul described them, "ever learning, and never able to come to the knowledge of the truth" (2 Tim. 3:7).

What a reproach to the Good Shepherd. He promises not only a search, but satisfaction.

A balanced life requires not only restlessness, but rest.

There must be not only aspiration but achievement. In a football game, if someone keeps moving the goal posts each time we get close to them, who would want to keep charging down the field?

In this one verse of Psalm 23, we can observe three things:

1. The guidance that brings fulfillment.
2. The satisfaction that brings rest.
3. The rest that brings renewal.

A strange reversal has come in our world. Missiles are guided and people are left to have their own way.

As I passed by the bookstore this week, I noticed a gigantic promotion for a new book *My Way: The Unofficial Biography of Frank Sinatra.* While I have not read the book or made a serious study of Mr. Sinatra's life, I suspect that the title is well chosen. That in itself is not bad. What is bad is that Mr. Sinatra is being admired as a lad who rose from obscurity to fame—and he did it "his way."

He has no monopoly on this approach. It is the way of the world, and the way of wayward sheep. Left to themselves, sheep wander into the den of wolves or into the barren mountainsides where even wolves disdain to go. "All we like sheep have gone astray: we have turned everyone to his own way," Isaiah said (53:6).

Independence leads not to fulfillment but frustration. Experience is an effective but tardy teacher. We learn, indeed, but too late.

Observation is often better than experience. Gary Moore used to remind me, "Learn from the mistakes of others; you don't have time to make all the mistakes yourself."

Unfortunately, even the experience of others cannot prepare us for the future. Nobody's world is quite like ours.

As my wife Berny and I prepared to leave Daytona Beach after being pastor for twenty-one years, the people expressed their regret at our leaving. One charming woman, wishing to show her love for us, said, "Who will we ever get to fill Brother Berquist's shoes?"

"That won't be a problem," Berny answered. "He is taking his shoes with him."

So do we all. No one can walk the path that we must walk. Neither their experience nor advice can really be ultimately helpful. In David's psalm, sheep are encouraged to follow the shepherd, not other sheep.

A bumper sticker on the back of a dusty green Chevrolet said: DON'T FOLLOW ME, I'M LOST.

That makes sense. But if all the lost Chevrolets could form a committee, make up a set of bylaws, and develop a logo, they would doubtless get a following. People are looking for guidance, even from doubtful sources.

Recently a sultry film star said, "I think I know something about marriage; I have been married five times."

What amazing logic! It is almost as though a business counseling service were to advertise for customers by listing the times it had gone bankrupt.

"Management by objective" has become the current style for

today's business world. Setting goals becomes the accepted procedure for every organization and every person within them. It all seems so logical and, well, so efficient that anyone challenging the system is about as popular as a motion to raise taxes.

And how do we set goals? Either by experience or speculation. Both are faulty.

Can you imagine a society of caterpillars adopting goals for the year? "Mr. Chairperson, I propose for this year that we crawl thirty percent faster than last year."

"Is that a motion? And is there a second?"

Such goals would be ambitious, but they would not be realistic. What would happen if a zealous caterpillar proposed, "I am not satisifed with this goal. I believe that we can fly on wings as beautiful as oriental lace. I think we can move into the world of space and leave the crawling to the earthworms."

"An interesting idea, Brother Caterpillar, but we must set goals that are logical and reachable."

To my knowledge, such meetings are not held in the world of our woolly friends. They are guided by a divine destiny—a destiny that includes far more than their logic could suggest. Only humans have the option of ignoring divine guidance. Only humans can ask for it. Only humans need to.

What we desperately need is guidance. The goals are in the mind of our Creator and they are far grander than we would choose for ourselves. It is doubtful we would believe them if God were foolish enough to reveal them to us. Instead of explaining his purposes to us, God chooses to ask for our simple trust. If you follow my guidance, he says, you will realize my objectives. There is no other way. If you choose not to follow, I will never tell you what you missed—it would be too painful.

Chapter 13:

In Quietness—
Strength

If you are traveling across the desert and see a village ahead, you may be sure of water. Life does not exist without it.

As the shepherd plans for his sheep, he must seek not only green pastures, but water as well. Seventy percent of the sheep's body weight is water. As in human beings, the body fluids keep nutrients flowing to all parts of the anatomy. Dehydration means death.

For the sheep, water is supplied as the shepherd discovers streams trickling down the mountainside. Or he may find pools of water held in rocky caverns. Sometimes, when no snow is melting and no rain is falling, sheep may even subsist on the dew that covers the meadows in the early morning.

When dew is the only source of moisture, the shepherd will rouse the sheep early, even against their will, to make sure that they have the dews of the morning. If he waits, the sun will evaporate the dew and the sheep will have nothing to drink.

What a parable for believers! How special are the morning hours before the heat of the day and the pressures of work drain the freshness from the mind. It is no secret that great saints have followed the example of Jesus, who "rose a great while before day and went into a solitary place and there prayed."

The land of the Bible is not well provided with waterways. To my knowledge, there were no bridges at all in Israel until the Allenby bridge was built across the Jordan River at the close of World War II. The word *bridge* does not occur in the Bible. The Jordan River is the only one large enough to require a bridge.

Even so, there are hidden springs, streams, and pools. A good shepherd knows them well.

Sometimes, when a stream is found, the shepherd has to construct a dam to make a pool so that the sheep can drink. Sheep will not drink from rushing waters.

Instinctively sheep fear streams because if they were to wade into the water, their absorbent wool would weight them down and the stream would carry them away. Little wonder they look for still waters.

Again, a lesson for us. Rushing streams turn the wheels of the mills, but quiet pools reflect the beauty of the heavens. Even the smallest pool can reflect the infinite sky.

Learning the value of stillness is one of the early lessons of those who follow the Good Shepherd.

Quite a few years ago, I wrote lyrics for a song whose first stanza begins "God speaks loudest in the silence."

Now, years later, I try to remember the ways God has led me. Usually this leadership did not come when I was busily telling him of my plans, but when I was quietly waiting for God to tell me his plans.

If we complain that God does not speak to us, it may be that he is simply waiting for our silence—a break in the conversation. Have you ever met someone who asked questions but never gave a chance for you to answer? Silence is that opportunity.

How quickly we are embarrassed when our worship services

have more than a few seconds of silence. You can almost hear a ripple of whispers across the congregation, "Why doesn't somebody do something?"

In our hearts, we know that we need to take time to hear from our heavenly Father, but when the time comes during the night and sleep is taken from us, we rush to the medicine chest to find something to get us back into unconsciousness.

Sometimes sickness slows us down. But instead of using those "still waters" for times of reflection, we fill the time with complaining.

Since we find it difficult to program quietness into our schedules, God finds a way.

George Mueller of Bristol, England, prayed for a million dollars for his orphanage in a day when a million dollars was a vast amount of money. He learned many of the deep secrets of prayer—particularly answered prayer. Out of his experience, he shared this truth:

> The Bible says that the steps of a good
> man are ordered of the Lord.
> I have found that the "stops" of a good man may
> also be ordered by the Lord.

In my own life, I have come to treasure the stops, the interruptions, as opportunities to listen to the Good Shepherd. Psalm 23 has become a favorite. I repeat it when I am on the six-lane freeway, in hopelessly snarled traffic. I repeat it when I am forced to wait for an appointment. I repeat it when I wake at night.

When the rushing waters of my life are stilled, I remember that God has promised to lead me to them. When I remember (and I must confess that I do not always remember) I relax and listen.

Who knows what fulfillment we could find if we would live our lives according to God's laws of harmony. In a musical score, the rests as well as the notes make the melody.

Unfortunately, most of us have not learned to rest without feeling guilty. Even our vacations are frantic efforts to meet schedules, cover miles, and accomplish goals. Little wonder that we need a vacation to recover from our vacation.

The Christian Sabbath is one of the most poorly understood teachings in the Bible. Not only is it important for us to have a day of physical rest, but it is even more important to have spiritual rest. Just as God rested from his labors after six days of creation, it is necessary for us to cease from our labors. Faith assures us that the work of redemption is done. We can rest in the knowledge that he "is able to keep that which has been committed unto him." Our salvation will not be made more complete by our anxiety.

Sabbath means rest. We need to enter it.

The importance of rest is now being researched by educators. In a recent book *Super Learning,* Sheila Ostrander and Lynn Schroeder tell about students' learning difficult languages such as Chinese and Arabic in thirty days. Easier languages, like Spanish, can be learned in ten days.

What is their secret of these amazing feats?

Rhythm. Interspersing rest with learning. Facts are fed to the student, then silence. Then more facts. Then more silence. Experiments have proved that musical accompaniment can be helpful. Baroque music has been found to be best, rock music the worst.

Sustained intensity will not work. A pause between ideas is important.

Our creator knows this. The beating of the heart—that marvelous fist-sized muscle—is an example. Every twenty-three seconds, your heart pumps blood through sixty thousand miles of arteries, veins, and capillaries. Without complaint, it works all your life. But it rests between beats. It has its own quiet time.

When your heart panics and beats wildly, without control, death becomes a threat.

The physical need of rest is so obvious that it seems unnecessary to write about it. But rest to our spirits is important, too. In fact, the two ideas are related.

Stressed and "driven" people need to be led.

How easy it is to imagine that God has deserted us when we see no visible signs of progress. When the charts do not climb and the graphs show no gain, we complain, Where is God?

The psalmist reminds us. He is still leading us beside still waters.

64

He restoreth my soul.
—Psalm 23:3

Chapter 14:

Relief for Starving Souls

I am writing these words in Kansas City, Missouri. While trying to hide in my motel room and write, I am occasionally distracted by kind friends who want to show me the local attractions. My problem is complicated because I actually enjoy being distracted.

Yesterday's outing took me to a famous barbecue restaurant. Though located in one of the less elegant parts of Kansas City, Bryant's Barbecue is sought out by all classes of people. Our Toyota was outclassed by Cadillacs, Mercedes, and Rolls Royces. Approaching our restaurant, we passed another popular eating place. A rickety building, painted a billious green, carried the sign Ruby's Soul Food.

"That's a good place," Greg said.

"What do they serve?"

"Actually, they serve good home-cooking. Southern cooking. Ham hocks and beans, black-eyed peas and collard greens, and stuff like that. You get all you want."

We didn't stop to sample Ruby's Soul Food (although I must admit I was tempted), but my mind buzzed with questions. What is soul food? What, in fact, is the soul?

If, as David says, it needs to be restored, from what has it fallen? What was it originally? How can it regain what it has lost?

Whether or not sheep have souls, David is convinced that he had a soul. He is convinced, too, that his soul is a very important part of his life. In fact, it may be his life.

In Psalm 42:11, he cried out:

> Why art thou cast down, O my soul
> and why art thou disquieted within me?

That David should speak of his soul's being "cast down" is not surprising. *Cast down* is a shepherd's term. A sheep may lie on his back to rest and then discover that he cannot get up again. His four legs are up in the air, pawing furiously, but they cannot help him. If he is lying in a low place, getting up becomes even more difficult.

If no one comes to help this "cast" sheep, the situation becomes worse. Blood drains from the legs, making them weaker. Body gases form within the sheep, crowding the vital organs. Unless someone comes to help, he will die.

The shepherd knows this danger, and so he watches carefully. Whenever he finds a "cast" sheep, he straddles it, lifts it, and helps it to stand. Sometimes he must massage the sheep's legs to restore circulation. Even when on its feet again, the sheep may stumble and fall. Patiently the shepherd must restore the animal.

We know these facts about sheep. What about people?

David himself had been "cast down." In a moment of weakness he had given in to temptation—the temptation of adultery with Bathsheba, the wife of another man. The sin was covered by another: murder. An avalanche of family problems followed.

In desperation, David realized that he could not help himself. Even though he was king, he was powerless to restore his soul, his life. Psalm 51 gives an insight into his desperate hunger for help.

Purge me with hyssop, and I shall be clean:
wash me, and I shall be whiter than snow.
Make me to hear joy and gladness;
that the bones which thou has broken may rejoice.
Hide thy face from my sins,
and blot out all mine iniquities.
Create in me a clean heart, O God;
and renew a right spirit within me.
Cast me not away from thy presence;
and take not thy holy spirit from me.
Restore unto me the joy of thy salvation;
and uphold me with thy free spirit.

—Psalm 51:7-11

See the pictures forming in David's mind? He sees himself not as a king robed in purple, but as a pitiful, sick man. His soul is sick. He sees himself as a sheep—a lost sheep—"cast down" and unable to put himself back on his feet.

Restoration is needed, restoration of the soul. And it must come from the outside. He cannot do it himself.

Following this experience, David's care of his soul becomes very important. Listen to him sing:

Bless the Lord, O my soul

and

My soul shall make her boast in the Lord.

Like David, we desperately need to think about our souls. In this age of cosmetic religion, we are tempted to be satisfied with "looking good." But God wants to begin his work on the inside.

Harry Emerson Fosdick once said, "The soul of a revolution is always the revolution of a soul." Change begins there.

Truthfully we should not say "I have a soul" but rather that "I am a soul." The Bible says this: "man became a living soul" (Gen. 2:7).

Any school child knows that our bodies are composed of dust—the elements of the earth: iron, phosphorous, calcium, zinc, manganese, and copper. But all of us know that we are more than a test tube full of mineral elements. Instinctively we know that we are "soul" as well.

A simple test proves the soul's existence: nourish your body without nourishing your spiritual nature and your body will suffer. Your soul will cry for help.

What a pathetic sight to see people trying to nourish their spiritual nature by pouring more and more into their bodies. Whether it is the wino on the street carrying cheap liquor in a brown paper bag or a jeweled socialite sipping liqueur from a crystal goblet, the problem is the same.

Consider the frustrated overweight Christian whose weapon is not a drug syringe, but a knife and fork. He tries to feed the loneliness of the soul by stuffing the body. A common practice, but deadly.

What is this soul of which David speaks? Jesus speaks of it:

> What is a man profited if he shall gain the whole
> world, and lose his own soul? or what shall a man
> give in exchange for his soul?
> —Matthew 16:26

In most Bibles, there is a marginal reading. The alternate word for *soul* is "life."

About nine-tenths of the mind is subconscious. Like an iceberg that is mostly submerged, the greater part of our mind is hidden from us. Planted in this part of our mind are memories, feelings, emotions, and images.

God wants to work in this part of our lives. It is here that God can do his most effective work. For locked within this subconscious mind, this soul, are guilt, failures, and bad memories. Hidden also in this soul are poor self-images given to us by unthinking parents or jealous friends.

A thousand chambered prisons exist in the soul. Small wonder that it is cast down.

The soul cries desperately to be restored, to be filled again with joy.

Desperate as is the cry of the soul, it is no less urgent than the invitation of God, who wants to restore the soul. He wants to lead us to become the person he planned for us to be. No matter how much the world on the outside changes, little lasting change can come in our lives until this soul is restored—until God gives back what it has lost.

Like a shepherd who gently lifts a "cast" sheep, God will lift us. He will massage our spindly self-image and restore circulation of new thoughts and dreams. He will watch as we take the first timid steps into a new life—and if we fall God will pick us up again. Shattered by rejection and failure, our confidence will become strong once more. If we have been told by our earthly parents "that we will never amount to anything," we will remember that there is a heavenly Father who really knows what we can do. And he is leading us, not into frustration because of impossible goals, but to fulfillment and to success.

Contemporary humorist Erma Bombeck has written a book titled *If Life Is a Bowl of Cherries, What Am I Doing in the Pits?* Her question has apparently spoken to many people—enough to make her book a bestseller.

Her question, however, comes three thousand years late. David asked the question. He knew despair, but he also knew deliverance. He could sing:

> He brought me up also out of a horrible pit,
> out of the miry clay,
> and set my feet upon a rock,
> and established my goings.
> And he hath put a song in my mouth,
> even praise unto our God.
> —Psalm 40:2-3

When people today find themselves "in the pits," they need a shepherd; they cannot lift themselves. The Judean sheep is a pitiful sight cast down, lying on its back and furiously pawing the air in an attempt to get back on its feet. The sheep needs a shepherd and knows it. More pitiful than this is the stress-ridden businessman or -woman, frustrated parent, or the intense student poring over self-help books, trusting in them to lift her or his spirits. She or he needs a shepherd. And it is not likely the person will find one—or be found of one—until she or he is willing to be a sheep, a follower.

God is waiting for that moment of truth.

He leadeth me in the paths of righteousness for his name's sake.

—Psalm 23:3

Chapter 15:

God Will Show You His Paths, But Never His Plans

Sheep are notorious path-takers. Once they have walked on a trail, they will take it again and again until the path becomes a gully. When the rains come, this gully becomes a rivulet, washing away the soil.

Displaying the herd instinct, sheep follow other sheep. Humans are not immune to this practice, either. "Everyone is doing it" seems to be justification for everything from wearing outlandish clothes to adopting the latest immoral life-style. The Bible warns us against doing this kind of conformity:

Thou shalt not follow a multitude to do evil.
—Exodus 23:2

71

Again, "Wide is the gate, and broad is the way, that leadeth to destruction, and many there be which go in thereat" (Matthew 7:13).

What is the alternative to this self-destructive pattern? Quite obviously it is to be led by the Good Shepherd into a path that may be lonely and individualistic, but one that leads to fulfillment and satisfaction.

In Bible lands, shepherding is a recognized profession, and only if people keep a good reputation for caring for both the sheep and the lands on which they pasture will they be steadily employed. Shepherds feel this responsibility keenly.

Just as in cattle-growing states of America animals are branded with their owner's mark, so in Bible lands sheep are marked. With a sharp knife, the shepherd cuts a particular kind of notch in the sheep's ear that is its brand. It denotes ownership, and ownership is very important.

Throughout this book I have stressed the importance of the *I*—the person. God truly wants to work with persons, to bring each to his or her maximum fulfillment, to realization of the dreams God actually had for us before we were even born. Second, life is constantly changing, either for better or worse. No one is locked into the past; nor can anyone live in the future. Third, millions of people spend their lives trying to find out who they are. The problem would be simple if they would find out *whose* they are. Our lives belong to God.

That is why self-surrender is the key to self-fulfillment. This surrender does not mean throwing ourselves like a limp noodle at the feet of God and saying, I'm yours. Do what you want with me.

Belonging to God means that we actively let God lead us. We seek God's direction, we look for God's paths.

We do not know how long it took David to learn that he was not smart enough to run his own life or his own kingdom. We only know that somewhere, after bitter failure, David discovered this principle of God's ownership. He knew he belonged to God.

Know ye that the Lord he is God: it is he that hath made us, and not we ourselves; we are HIS people, and the sheep of HIS pasture.
—Psalms 100:3 (emphasis added)

In times of prosperity and success, we easily take control of our lives and credit for our success. In times of trouble we readily look for someone to blame—even God. How much simpler it would be for us to move under God's orders all the time, for God is willing to take responsibility for any life that he directs. Then, when trouble comes, God is able to deliver his child.

The Apostle Paul began his career fighting God's battles for him. The only mistake was that he was directing his own life. Later, and painfully, he learned to submit to God. But what assurance this gave the missionary apostle! Observe his calmness when all his friends panicked.

Paul was a prisoner on a ship headed eventually for Italy. God revealed to him that the ship should delay the journey because of stormy weather. When Paul told the owners about God's message, they rejected it and insisted on setting sail as they had originally planned.

Soon, just as Paul predicted, the storm did come and the crew took desperate measures to save the ship. They threw cargo and tackling overboard. For many days neither sun nor stars appeared. Finally Paul spoke to the officers and the crew:

> I exhort you to be of good cheer; for there shall be no loss of any man's life among you, but of the ship. For there stood by me this night the angel of God, whose I am, and whom I serve, saying, Fear not.
> —Acts 27:22, 23

The key to Paul's confidence—and ours—lies in the phrase "whose I am and whom I serve." Just as the owners of the ship could make a decision about it, so God could take charge of Paul's destiny since Paul had given him ownership.

The idea occurs again and again in Paul's letter to the young churches of Asia:

> You are not your own; you were bought with a price.
> So glorify God in your body.
> —1 Corinthians 6:20

At an earlier time, Paul traveled to Damascus to imprison Christians. Energetically, he was trying to do what he thought

73

God wanted done. But God stopped him. Struck down and blinded, Paul finally asked the question that changed his life: "Lord, what wilt thou have me to do?"

Paul's rugged confidence in the face of the storm did not come from his seamanship, but from his surrender. He belonged to God, and therefore his path—even the stormy path of the sea—was God's path.

Why did this happen? Who knows? God does not show us his plans, only his path. If we do not follow God's path we will never learn his plans. All of us would like for him to show us the plans so that we could decide whether or not we wanted to follow his path, but God doesn't work that way.

David knew this:

> Thy word is a lamp unto my feet, and a light unto my path.
>
> —Psalm 119:105

Guessing the future is an age-old pastime. Ancient but futile. Mature believers know that God will direct us, but God will illuminate only the step ahead, not the distant future. We are promised enough light to walk in, but not enough to speculate about.

As one wit put it, "The parts of the Bible that trouble me are not those I cannot understand, but the part I understand clearly but find difficult to obey."

Obedience today is a guarantee for guidance tomorrow. Disobedience means darkness.

What a privilege to choose to follow God's guidance.

In his excellent book *A Shepherd Looks at Psalm 23,* Phillip Keller tells of keeping a flock of sheep on his luxuriant pasturelands. The fields next to his belonged to an absentee owner. The hireling shepherd took little care of the pastures, so they were brown and barren, while Keller's were lush and green.

The sheep on the barren pastures became gaunt and sickly. Through bleary and watery eyes they looked longingly at the lush clover and grass of Keller's fields. They tried desperately to crawl under the wire fence to satisfy their hunger. They longed, I am sure, to change owners. But they could not.

Not true of us. We can choose the person to whom we belong.

74

In fact we must choose. God will not choose for us.

Interesting that the first words of Psalm 23 are "The Lord is my shepherd."

A choice has been made. When we choose to belong to God, all other blessings can come to us. Eventually we can say with David, "I will dwell in the house of the Lord forever." But the original choice is ours. God is eager to claim us, to guide us, and to provide for us. He wants to speak lovingly of us as "my sheep," but he cannot do this until we say "my shepherd."

Listing the three giant steps from *I* to *IS* to *HIS* may take less than one line of print, but actually taking the steps may take a long time. The journey, however, shouldn't be as long as most of us make it. And it may not be as easy as we would wish it. But, considering the alternative, the choice shouldn't be hard.

Actually, it shouldn't be postponed.

Yea, though I walk through the valley of the shadow of death, I will fear no evil.
                                    —Psalm 23:4

Chapter 16:

Where Is the Good Shepherd in Bad Times?

Shortly after I had fastened my seatbelt for take-off, I noticed that the passenger beside me had already opened a book and had begun to read. I glanced at the title *When Bad Things Happen to Good People.*

When the woman next to me noticed my interest, she said, "I bought this book for my sister. Her child is terminally ill and she can't imagine why anything like this should come to her family."

Rabbi Harold Kushner, the author of the book she was reading, asked the same question. Faced with the incurable illness of his son, he found himself looking at people who apparently had no interest in God. They lived simply for themselves. Yet their children were healthy while his son was dying.

We have all asked questions like these. Why cannot life be made up of mountaintop experiences? Why do we have sickness, pain, and defeat? Does God love us during these times? Does he lead us into them?

Our brain tells us yes, but our emotions cry out maybe.

Phillip Yancey asks the same question in his book *Where Is God When It Hurts?*

Surely sheep ask the same questions when they follow their shepherd into the steep mountain trails. Panting and struggling for footing, they wonder why the man who has provided for them so well in the lowlands would take them to such rugged terrain. They have no choice. They must trust the shepherd. He is leading them to new pastures, but he cannot explain what he is doing.

Every mountain has its valleys. Glaciers and streams cut deep wounds in the mountainsides. Crevices and gorges scar the rocky slopes. But every climber knows that passing through these valleys is the only way to reach the top.

In the world of shepherding, the shepherd must find new ranges for his flock. In the summer months he takes them to the highlands. This is not without danger. Sudden storms, wild animals, rock slides, and avalanches threaten. But there is no other way to new pasturelands—the valley is the only road. In Psalm 23, this is known as "the valley of the shadow of death."

At this point in David's picturesque psalm, a wonderful change occurs. Speaking of the Good Shepherd in the earlier verses, David uses the third person pronoun *he,* referring, of course, to God. Now, in the dark valley, the pronoun changes to second person, *thou.* David has moved from interest in God to intimacy with God:

Thou art with me, thy rod and thy staff they comfort me.

In the valley we do not talk about God, we talk to God. And he talks to us. It is *I* and *thou* or more commonly, *me* and *you.*

This may well be the distinction between religion and vital experience with God. On the one hand we have theory, on the other, trust.

Some time ago, I rode up Lakeshore Drive in Chicago with a nationally known journalist and newscaster. Throughout his life, fortune has smiled on him. Though still a young man, he enjoys exciting work and is handsomely paid for it.

As we rode, he began speaking.

This has been the most difficult month of my life. Incredible pressures have come with my job. My father is dying of cancer, and I have just learned that my wife also has cancer and must undergo radical surgery. I have been backed up to the wall. But during this month I have discovered that when I reach the end of my understanding, God is there. I have learned something about God that I did not know before, although I have been a believer since childhood: God is especially present in hard places.

Sheep may wander when the sun is shining, but when the sky grows dark they huddle close to their shepherd. When they hear the growling of wild animals, they nudge closer and closer to their guide.

It seems to me that we do not adequately prepare people for trouble. Somehow they are led to believe that the way of faith is a flower-strewn, red-carpeted, well-marked path.

Every saint knows that it is not.

Two children were making their way up the mountainside. The little girl was having trouble with the rough rocks. "I wish it would all be smooth," she said.

"The rough places are what you climb on," answered her brother.

We all wish it would be smooth, but looking back on our lives we realize that much of our progress has been made through pain. Perhaps we should thank God for failures. What do we learn from success?

Admiring the success of celebrities, how easy it is to view them enviously on the pinnacle of fame and ignore the rocky path by which they reached this height!

A few months ago I found myself in the Calgary, Alberta, Canada airport. While I sat in the waiting room writing letters, I heard music, unmistakably bagpipes, playing.

I followed the sound of the Scotch melodies and soon was a part of a crowd of thousands who had come to welcome the

Olympic athletes. Among the winners were two young female swimmers who had dazzled the world with their precision and skill.

Television cameras poked through the crowd. Home-made banners unfurled. Eager hands reached out to touch the celebrities. Autograph books and pieces of paper were thrust out for signatures. The girls were avalanched with attention.

Excitement was electric. The girls enjoyed the welcome—as indeed they should. As I watched, I remembered reading of the thousands of hours these young women had practiced their routines. No one cheered as they passed through the valley of self-denial, pushing themselves relentlessly. No one urged them on as they disciplined themselves without mercy.

Mountaintops there are in this world, but few are undeserved.

Psalm 23 has been called "The Nightingale of the Psalms." It has earned this title. Throughout the darkest night the nightingale sings. No night, no song.

To understand the origin of David's song, we must look at the psalm that precedes it, Psalm 22.

> My God, my God, why has thou forsaken me? why art thou so far from helping me, and from the words of my roaring? O my God, I cry in the daytime, but thou hearest not; and in the night season, and am not silent (vv. 1-2).

Surely this psalm describes one of the valleys David passed through. We know that it speaks of the valley that Jesus, the Great Shepherd, would pass through. These are the words that came from his parched lips as he hung on a cross.

> My God, My God, why has thou forsaken me?

David learned, as we do, that God does not desert us when we are in difficult times.

Does this "valley of the shadow of death" refer only to difficult things in life, or does it actually talk of the time when we shall come to the end of our earthly life?

It speaks of both.

When shadows gather and you realize that what you have

known of life is ending, and you are facing a new reality, a new world, you do not need to face it alone. There will be what ancient saints have called a "dying grace." You do not need it until you die. But when you are dying, if you have chosen the Lord for your shepherd, grace will be there when you need it, and so will the Lord.

On the other hand, if you have chosen to go your own way, stumbling from disappointment to disappointment, from frustrated dream to failure, it is not likely that you will have confidence in the hour of death. Grace—living grace and dying grace—are options.

The choice is yours.

Thy rod and thy staff they comfort me.
—Psalm 23:4

Chapter 17:

When The Gentle Shepherd Isn't Gentle

In a lifetime of traveling, I have collected only a few souvenirs. For part of my life, I was an unmarried transient, going wherever my limited funds and unlimited curiosity would take me. I bought souvenirs, but I gave them to my friends who had homes in which to display them. My only home was a battered brown suitcase, covered with stickers. It had no room for copper teapots or embroidered tapestries.

One souvenir has survived: a knob-kerrie from Africa. The knob-kerrie is the shepherd's rod.

Whenever you see a shepherd, anywhere in the world, you find him carrying two things: a rod and a staff. Modern shepherds carry rifles instead of a club, but the purpose is the same.

In Africa, where I first encountered a shepherd's club, I noticed that both men and boys approaching manhood would not be without it. When a boy was old enough to carry a club, he was first assigned to the job of making it.

Finding a young tree, he would uproot it and then fashion a knob-kerrie from it. The large knot at the root of the tree became a ball-like handle for the club. The long part of the club would be fashioned from the trunk of the sapling. Great care was taken in shaping and polishing the club.

Having made his club, the lad would then learn to use it, spending long hours throwing it at a target, much as American boys are taught to throw a baseball.

Speed and accuracy were important. If a snake should appear in the path, the club could quickly kill it. If the enemy were not directly underfoot, the club would be thrown. The knob-kerrie was an extension of the owner's right arm.

In David's time, it was not uncommon for the club to have an iron spike in it, making it even more deadly.

What comfort the sheep must have found by looking at this club. They remembered David's killing a lion and a bear with this weapon. If other wild beasts attacked, the shepherd could deal with them as well. Once again the expertly hurled club could find its target.

David calls it "thy rod." It is interesting to note how this term has crept into modern speech. Western cattle ranchers riding the range do not carry sticks of wood to protect their herds. Handguns, pistols, and revolvers are used. Often these are called "rods." The purpose has not changed in three thousand years—comfort and security.

Reading Psalm 23, we can see that the shepherd's rod does two things: it deals with the sheep's enemies and it disciplines the sheep themselves.

Wise sheep appreciate both functions.

What are our enemies today? Sometimes they are real, and sometimes imagined. But the paralyzing fear that comes with them is the same.

Some time ago I received a phone call from Robert Jones, a social worker in the National Institute of Health in Bethesda, Maryland. He had read the book Charles Schulz and I worked on,

The Doctor Is In, and he wanted to meet me.

He said, "One of our patients, Robert Hirt of Norfolk, Virginia, brought some of your books to the hospital and has been sharing them with the patients. I read a copy and found it helpful in counseling other patients. If you ever get to Washington, I would like to meet you."

As it happened, I was to be in Washington, D.C., and made it a point to go to NIH, the largest cancer research hospital in the world. Mr. Jones took me through the facility.

"Mr. Berquist," he began, "here at the National Institute of Health, we are surrounded by the newest and most powerful methods of treating cancer. Everything that science has discovered about treatment is being used here.

"However, we are not always successful. About 50 percent of the patients are cured. The other 50 percent lose the battle against cancer.

"It is not surprising that many families request an autopsy to discover the actual cause of death. What is amazing is that we often discover that, although the patient died, the cancer was cured. He died from lack of hope. The six letter word *cancer* was too big for him to handle. He lost hope.

"With all their skill, our doctors and pharmacists cannot develop a capsule of hope that can be taken three times a day. Your book gives that kind of hope."

Naturally I was delighted to know that a book of mine had ministered to terminally ill people. But this conversation with Robert Jones took on an even greater meaning a short time later. Jeannie Jones called from Florida.

Jeannie is a nurse who worked with my wife, Berny, in Halifax Medical Center. In the course of their friendship, Jeannie had become a radiant Christian.

Although Jeannie had believed in Christ as the Son of God, she never really had a personal experience with him; she had never asked for his daily guidance. When she made that decision, her life took on a new meaning.

Then came the dark valley.

While we were living in Indiana, Jeannie called us. "I have really been through something new," she began. "A while back, I began to feel bad and finally entered the hospital for tests and eventually surgery.

85

"When I came out of surgery, my doctor, Alvin Smith, said to me, 'Jeannie, I am going to level with you. You have cancer. You know that we will do everything that we can, but truthfully, there isn't much we can do for you. You are a nurse; you know what the usual time is.'

"After Doctor Smith had gone, I began to cry. I had talked about cancer, I had told patients of their cancers, but it's different when you have it. I lay on the bed, looked at the ceiling, and said, 'What a terrible six-letter word. C-A-N-C-E-R. I came into the hospital merely feeling bad. Now I have cancer.

"I kept looking up at the ceiling and said out loud, 'Cancer is a terrible six-letter word. But I know another six-letter word that is greater: C-H-R-I-S-T.' "

As I relate this story of Jeannie, I check the calendar and see that the experience took place more than four years ago. If today is normal, Jeannie is working from 3:00 to 11:00 at Halifax Medical Center. The Shepherd's rod had dealt with her enemy. She shares this comfort with others.

Paul had this kind of faith in the name of Jesus.

At the name of Jesus every knee shall bow,
of things in heaven, and things in earth,
and things under the earth.
—Philippians 2:10

Even the most malicious disease must bow before the power of Christ.

A recent book dealing with the emotional effects of illness, *Anatomy of an Illness* by Norman Cousins, advises cancer patients to imagine a war inside their bodies—a war in which a hungry goblin consumes the cancer cells, the enemy. Who can say if this kind of therapy works? Many patients claim that it does. If so, good. But Christians have a better answer. Their Good Shepherd can deal with the enemies. His rod and staff comfort me. This is not imaginary.

It may take imagination for us to visualize ourselves on the hillsides of Israel, sheep among the prowling predators, ravenous beasts, and poisonous snakes. But it does not take much imagination to think of the enemies that lurk in our jet-paced polyester world. Disease threatens the body, stress pressures the mind, and

86

politics empty our pocketbooks.

Feeling threatened is not a sign of mental illness. We actually are threatened. Peace of mind comes only when we remember that the Good Shepherd may be gentle with us, but he is ruthless with our enemies. How often we ought to sing, "Thy rod and thy staff, they comfort me."

While the sheep rejoice that their shepherd is able to hurl his rod at their natural enemies, they remember that he is also able to throw the rod at a sheep that is wandering—getting out of reach.

Sometimes when a sheep is getting close to a precipice or is about to be attacked by an unseen foe, the shepherd is too far away to reach with his arm, his crooked staff, or even his voice. He must hurl the club.

Temporarily stunned by this unexpected attack from the gentle shepherd he has come to trust, the sheep will turn and come running back from danger.

Jesus may have been thinking of this kind of protection when he taught us to pray, "Deliver us from evil."

How does God rescue us from danger today? What is his rod— the extension of the Good Shepherd's arm?

Scripture. The written word of God is the disciplining rod. As we listen to God's Word, we are reproved and exhorted. D.L. Moody, the effective evangelist of years gone by, is quoted as saying,

> The Bible will keep you from sin,
> or sin will keep you from the Bible.

Getting a whack on the side of the head by a direct application of Scripture is never pleasant, but it is better than being a picnic lunch for wolves.

Discipline is an evidence of God's love.

> My son, despise not the chastening of the Lord, nor faint when thou art rebuked of him. For whom the Lord loveth he chasteneth, and scourgeth every son whom he receiveth.
>
> —Hebrews 12:5

A third function of the rod is to bring healing. The heavy wool

87

that covers the sheep makes it difficult to see wounds or sores that could bring pain or even death. Consequently, the shepherd has the sheep pass under the rod. With the rod, he parts the wool, looks at the skin, and is able to know where to pour in the healing oil.

No wonder David, who had been disciplined by God, cried out for this kind of loving scrutiny:

Search me, O God, and know my heart:
try me, and know my thoughts:
And see if there be any wicked way in me,
and lead me in the way everlasting.
—Psalm 139:23, 24

David knew that not all adversaries are on the outside. Certainly the Good Shepherd can deal with external foes, but his rod can also reveal hidden enemies. The psalmist found comfort in this fact. And so may we.

We have talked at length about the rod; what about the staff?

In modern times, rifles and revolvers may have replaced the shepherd's rod, but the staff remains his principal, tool—his trademark. In Christmas pageants, for example, shepherds are rarely equipped with a rod, but always with a staff.

No one needs to be told what a staff looks like, but it may be helpful to talk about its use. The crook on the long staff is designed to fit either around the sheep's neck or his foreleg. Sometimes when the shepherd is trying to train a young lamb, he will place the crook of his staff around the lamb's neck, forcing him to stay near.

For some reason, sheep sometimes tend to disown their families. The shepherd knows that they must stay together whether they want to or not. An experienced shepherd knows that once the mother sheep becomes accustomed to the scent of her lamb, she will accept him and keep him with her.

Here is surely a parable for modern Christians who demonstrate a mania for division!

Can we hear the Good Shepherd say once again, "Jerusalem, Jerusalem . . . how often would I have gathered thy children together"? (Matthew 23:37).

Or again, "Other sheep I have, which are not of this fold: them also I must bring . . . and there shall be one fold, and one shepherd" (John 10:16).

Nowhere is the shepherd's love for his sheep more clearly shown than in his going after the wandering lamb. If through his own carelessness a sheep has fallen into a crevice in the rock, the shepherd can reach down with his staff and lift it out. If the sheep has not fallen but is wandering too far from the flock, the shepherd can reach with his staff and pull him back.

Two teen-agers were sitting in a roadside tavern. The hour was late. "I'd better be getting home," one said. "I hate it, but my parents won't rest until I get home."

"I sure wish mine felt that way," responded the other young man wistfully. "My folks don't care."

Not only does God care for his sheep, Jesus said, but the Good Shepherd would give his life for them. He not only searches for them, but he searches until he finds them. His rod and his staff are able to deal both with the sheep and their enemies.

That is a great comfort.

Thou preparest a table before me in the presence of mine enemies.

—Psalm 23:5

Chapter 18:

The Wolf Who Came to Dinner

In his eagerness to nourish his sheep, the shepherd keeps looking for newer and greener fields. In some of the finest sheep countries in the world, the most lush pastures are in the mountains. After climbing wearily, the sheep come to these welcome flatlands. Protected by surrounding peaks and watered by mountain streams, these highland plateaus are ideal for summer feeding.

The table of which David speaks is such a place. When he writes "thou preparest a table before me" he is not thinking of a red checkered tablecloth and a wicker picnic basket, but a banquet, nonetheless.

In Spanish, these tablelands are called *mesas*. *Mesa* is also the common word for *table* in Swahili, the trade language of Africa.

It becomes obvious as we listen to David's song that God is eager to nourish his sheep. Wherever he has to lead them to feed them, he is willing to go.

His care is easily seen in all the world of nature. Tiny birds are provided complicated navigational wisdom to know when and where to fly so that they can be cared for. The little ants instinctively provide for winter. Animals that have to endure cold winters grow heavier coats. God loves the world of nature. But he loved people more.

Jesus said it:

> Are not two sparrows sold for a farthing? and one of them shall not fall on the ground without your Father.
> . . . Ye are of much more value than many sparrows.
> —Matthew 10:29, 31

David again puts things in perspective by talking of nature. Even though God cares for the animals, he gives people a higher priority.

> O fear the Lord, ye his saints: for there is no want to them that fear him. The young lions do lack, and suffer hunger: but they that seek the Lord shall not want any good thing.
> —Psalm 34:9, 10

In the world of the godless, little can be found to nourish the spirit. Children are told that the birth of humankind on this planet is an accident of nature. They are educated to believe that many years ago gases cooled to form elements of solid matter. In time, simple forms of animal life arose from these elements. After centuries these living creatures climbed out of the slime and into a world of people. According to this theory, people are no more important than the dust we wipe off our piano.

One pagan writer said, "Man is a monkey who chatters to himself about kinship with the angels and grovels in the earth for ground nuts."

Another pessimist declared, "Man is the scaly epidermis of a second-rate planet."

God does not feel this way about us. He wants to nourish our sense of self-worth. He wants the *I* that we can become to break out of the cocoon of what we have been.

Not only does the godless world taunt us with our humble origins, but it attacks our achievements. Criticism abounds. Even though we were created for fantastic achievement, we face misunderstanding of all kinds. When Ralph Waldo Emerson said, "To be great is to be misunderstood," he was speaking for his own encouragement as well as for ours.

Being misunderstood may be our only claim to greatness, but all of us are attacked by our friends as well as our enemies. And if that weren't enough, we proceed to find fault with ourselves.

Professional students of human nature tell us that the negative effects of criticism can be actually measured in our bodies and in our minds. Blood pressure, metabolism, and body temperature all respond negatively to criticism. They in turn injure our physical and mental health.

The end result: we become sick.

Even more shocking is that it takes five positive statements (such as compliments or congratulations) to overcome the effects of one critical remark. Small wonder that we need to have our spirits nourished, that we need to have the Good Shepherd prepare a table before us.

When we receive an invitation to the Lord's table, we are happy because then, at last, we are sure we will be free from our enemies. Not so, our enemies read our mail! Our enemies invite themselves.

Do you remember "Higher Ground," a popular song with Christians a generation ago? Doubtless the author had Psalm 23 in mind when he talked of a higher level of living:

My heart has no desire to stay
Where doubts arise and fears dismay;
Tho' some may dwell where these abound,
My prayer, my aim, is higher ground.

Lord, lift me up and let me stand,
By faith, on heaven's tableland.
A higher plane than I have found;
Lord, plant my feet on higher ground.

This is a good song. I still like it. But I am not sure that David would. When he talked of higher ground, it was in the presence of his enemies. Like ants, doubts and fears come to the picnic! It is easy to understand why David wrote, "Thou preparest a table before me in the presence of mine enemies."

A few years ago, my wife and I toured Kenya in Africa. One of the attractions everyone insisted we see was Tree-tops, a watering hole for animals. It was indeed a spectacular place.

A hotel is constructed on stilts so that tourists can watch as the wild animals come to the watering hole. The drama begins at dark. A large spotlight illuminates the pool so that guests can see the procession. First come tiny gazelles, then larger deer. Next, gnus and zebras and finally buffalo and elephants. Every animal in its fight for survival has to recognize the competition of its fellow animals. It comes to drink, but it must keep looking over its shoulder for someone larger than it is. This is the law of nature.

It is also a law of the spiritual world. The shepherd of David's psalm knew that sheep love the fresh green foliage of the mountainside, but he knew also that the wolves and lions love the tender meat of lambs.

So he had to protect his flock.

We would be foolish to imagine that our spiritual progress will be uncontested. Enemies may be within our home. Certainly they will be in the hostile world.

Of all the truths that have come to me in my study of God's leading his people to the Promised Land, the most surprising fact came to me late in life. What is it?

Canaan is full of Canaanites.

As a child I sang songs about the land of corn and wine, the land where God promised that everyone would live under his own vine and fig tree. The Hebrew Shangrila. Paradise.

Then I learned of the Canaanites, these terrible people who invented atrocious methods of torture for their enemies. Among these fierce peoples were Amorites, Hittites, Jebusites, and Philistines. Of course, God did promise to smite these enemies if his people would obey him. And he did. But without divine help, the dream of the Promised Land would have been a disaster.

Even Christ faced enemies. The story of his temptation describes the tension.

94

And he was there in the wilderness forty days, tempted of Satan; and was with the wild beasts; and the angels ministered unto him.

—Mark 1:13

Angels and animals. Satan and the Spirit. The battle never ends. The Good Shepherd has prepared a table before us. Guess who is coming to dinner. The enemy. But the Good Shepherd with his rod and with his word of power is there to keep peace and safety.

Thou anointest my head with oil.
—Psalm 23:5

Chapter 19:

God's Lambs and the Lamb of God

A shepherd on Israel's hillside travels light. He does not burden himself with excess baggage. Nevertheless, a few tools are always with him: the rod, the staff, and the bottle of oil. Anointing is an important part of his work.

In the same way that modern people feel a sense of protection when they pay premiums on their health insurance, sheep feel secure when they see the oil vial swinging from their shepherd's leather belt. They know healing is nearby.

Summertime is especially troublesome for sheep. As the warm sun and gentle showers make green fields and ideal growing conditions for the lambs, these same favorable factors encourage insects.

With summer come flies of all kinds: bot flies, heel flies, nasal flies, deer flies, black flies, and warble flies. Along with these flies are mosquitoes, gnats, and other troublesome parasites.

Swarms of insects can drive sheep to distraction. Worst among all the flies are the nose flies that breed in the nasal passages of the sheep. If these flies find their way into the nasal passages, they deposit eggs that will hatch into larvae in a few days. These larvae will then crawl up into the sheep's head.

In agony from this irritation, the sheep may beat his head against a rock, a tree, or the earth. Sheep have been known to kill themselves trying to rid themselves of this painful infestation. Even if the sheep survives the insects, the infection they caused may lead to blindness.

If you were to see a flock of sheep gamboling in the field, you might think they are feeling their oats. Actually they could be racing from place to place trying to avoid the ever-present insects.

The hazards of nature have turned the quiet pasture into a battleground.

A wise shepherd knows the danger. So at the first sign of insects, he begins to anoint the sheep with a special ointment. In Bible times the ointment was usually made of olive oil, sulphur, and aromatic spices. The mixture was liberally spread on the sheep's head—especially around the nose. In moments, relief would come, and the sheep could again graze peacefully in the green pastures. Anointing brought healing.

As David talked about his relationship with the Good Shepherd, he understood the importance of anointing. Though he was a king, David was troubled on every side.

Sometimes the enemies that destroy us are not big things, but microscopic irritations.

Petty troubles can drive us up the wall. They can make us want to bang our heads against a stone. Just as the sheep who has escaped the wolf is slain by a fly, tiny problems can destroy our peace of mind.

Often humble people imagine that those in places of power and wealth are free from petty problems. Those who have "arrived" know better. A former governor of Georgia knew that leaders are not exempt from problems. In fact, the greater one's responsibility, the greater the chance of problems. He said, "The fleas go with the dog. The bigger the dog, the more fleas." So it is not likely that any of us, however successful we may be, will avoid problems and vexations.

Does the Good Shepherd have an answer for these irritations? Yes. The Bible uses anointing oil as a symbol of the Holy Spirit—the very presence of God. Nowhere are we promised immunity from irritations. We are, however, promised that God's spirit will help us. He will heal our abrasions and wounds. He does indeed anoint our head with oil.

> For the promises of God . . . are yea, and in him Amen, unto the glory of God by us. Now he which stablisheth us with you in Christ, and hath anointed us, is God; Who hath also sealed us, and given us the earnest of the Spirit in our hearts.
>
> —2 Corinthians 1:20-22

Just when the sheep look longingly at the shepherd's vial of oil when they are being attacked by insects, so we should look longingly to God for his anointing.

Insects are not the only enemy of the sheep. A highly infectious scab can infect the flock. Since the sheep are heavily covered with wool, scab is not easily seen until it has already done much of its sinister work.

Again the shepherd uses his rod to push back the wool to look for these painful sores. When he finds them, he pours in the healing oil.

What a picture of the healing ministry of the Spirit!

In the rough-and-tumble world of business, in the day-by-day irritations of family living, in the abrasive pressures of city living, everyone gets hurt. Even the most superficial wounds can become infected if not healed.

Our pride makes us cover our wounds and we put on a brave face, even though we are deeply troubled. We are even tempted to conceal these hurts from God. Maybe our doctrine of the Holy Spirit keeps us from asking for help, since we profess to have him already!

Whatever our theological disagreements about the work of the Spirit, every honest person knows that he or she needs more than one anointing of the Holy Spirit. We need the constant presence of the Spirit—a fresh anointing.

Regardless of what happens, we must not let the Spirit depart. Paul warned us, "Grieve not the Holy Spirit, whereby ye are sealed unto the day of redemption" (Ephesians 4:30).

At least one other problem calls for a special anointing in the life of the sheep. Phillip Keller writes of this in his book *A Shepherd Looks at Psalm 23:*

> Sheep can attack each other.
> When the fly-infested summer is over, sheep enter the mating season. After early frosts have killed most of the insects that plague the outside of the woolly bodies, a new kind of feeling arises within. Male sheep, the rams, feel a surge of sexual power and begin to compete for the favors of females. They strut and preen. They grow jealous. And they are ready to do battle with other rams.

Sheep actually duel to win the right to a ewe. They butt heads, charging like knights of old. Sometimes the crash of heads and bodies can be heard echoing through the mountains.

The shepherd understands what is happening. He knows, too, that sheep can actually maim, cripple, or even kill one another in these fearsome battles. Consequently, in this season of the year, the shepherd will anoint the rams in a special way. He catches the arrogant rams and liberally smears their heads with grease.

The anointing does not change their nature, but it softens the blows. When they crash together, instead of injuring each other, they merely glance harmlessly off one another. After a few such futile attacks, they simply feel ridiculous. Their anger is diffused. Tension is gone. Little damage has been done.

While we like to think of sheep as gentle by nature, we know there is a pecking order in the world of animals. The desire for power exists in the world of sheep. One doesn't have to be a goat to feel like butting heads.

Among God's people there is abundant evidence of this same aggressiveness. Leaders emerge and threaten other leaders. In New Testament times, James and John wanted to sit on either side of Jesus when he came into power. The desire to be "top sheep" is not limited to the woolly world. It can invade boards of directors and women's auxiliaries, even children at play.

Wounds and even spiritual death can result from these struggles for power.

Sometimes persons on the outside of the Christian fellowship look with amusement on the fights within the flock and decide they do not need that kind of trouble.

Believers can become uncharitable, stiff-necked, and argumentative, all the while claiming to be "sheep of his pasture." Sheep may escape wolves only to be the victim of other sheep. Sad.

But anointing from the Holy Spirit resolves this problem. Frictions between people disappear when even one of the sparring members is adequately anointed.

Mechanics know the importance of anointing their engines. Without oil, even the best-engineered automobile would go only a few hundred yards. Properly lubricated, it will run for several hundred-thousand miles.

When we drive our cars to the service station to put gasoline in them, we are often asked, "Can I check your oil?" Translated into Bible language, the attendant is saying, "Is your engine properly anointed?"

This is a good question to ask ourselves as we undertake the work of any day.

The whole subject of anointing is fascinating, giving clues to the work of the Holy Spirit in the life of the believer. Yet another aspect of anointing is perhaps more important than any other. Anointing is the recognition of kingship.

Early in the Scriptures, we learn that priests and prophets were anointed with oil to show that they were chosen of God. Later anointing was also given to kings. The first king of Israel was Saul. Samuel the prophet was told to look for a man "who stood head and shoulders above his fellow men." Such a man would be looking for his father's lost animals.

"When you find him," Samuel was told, "you are to anoint him. He is my chosen king."

It happened just as God said. Saul found Samuel and asked help finding his lost animals. The prophet recognized Saul as the man God has described and immediately took him aside to anoint him.

Even though the people did not yet know what had happened, they had a king—God's choice. No banners flew, no bands played. There was no inauguration. There was simply the anointing—

Samuel poured oil on Saul's head.

Later David was anointed king of Israel. Saul had died, partly by falling on his spear and partly by the sword of an Amalekite— an enemy soldier. David was angered by the soldier's slaying of the king. Even though Saul had begged the soldier to kill him to relieve him of his self-inflicted pain, David did not feel that this was right. Even in death, Saul was God's anointed.

> How wast thou not afraid to stretch forth thine hand to destroy the Lord's anointed?
>
> —2 Samuel 1:14

A special protection comes from God's anointing. But we have not yet talked about the most important meaning of anointing. Anointing is not only a sign of Israel's kings—but the sign of the King of all Kings, the Lord of all Lords.

The word *Messiah* means "the anointed one."

Messiah is a Hebrew word. The same word in Greek, the language of the New Testament, is *Christ*.

The Old Testament tells of many kings who were anointed, but it prophesies about one whose kingdom would never end.

> Thy throne, O God, is forever and ever. . . . Therefore God . . . hath anointed thee with the oil of gladness above thy fellows.
>
> —Psalm 45:6, 7

Jesus claimed the title of Messiah. In speaking to the woman of Samaria, he said:

> I that speak unto thee am he.
> —John 4:26

We do not need to be scholars either of Hebrew or Greek to understand what Jesus was saying. We need only to read the conversation of this Samaritan woman. She was familiar with the first five books of the Bible, the books of Moses. She was acquainted with anointing. She knew there would one day be a specially anointed one to be called Messiah. She also knew the Greek word for this exalted one:

I know that Messias cometh, which is called Christ: when he is come, he will tell us all things.

—John 4:25

"I am the anointed one," Jesus said.

Jesus also said, "I am the good shepherd." As the Good Shepherd, he provides anointing for his sheep—he gives them the Holy Spirit. As he prepared to leave his disciples, knowing their anxiety, Jesus said:

It is expedient for you that I go away: for if I go not away, the Comforter will not come unto you; but if I depart, I will send him unto you.

—John 16:7

Following this line of thought, we easily see that anointing for the sheep of God's pasture not only heals their wounds and lubricates their human frictions; it also seals their relationship with the king. Being anointed, they now have a royal inheritance.

We are children of the heavenly kingdom.

With this in mind, let me tell you a story—a true story—that unlocks the meaning of anointing to me.

In Daytona Beach, Florida, I was principal of a Christian school. Occasionally I visited the classes. One day Martha Black asked me to come to her second-grade class to pray for a little girl.

This was a challenge. Although I believe strongly in healing, I was not sure I could make these second grade students understand it.

"This is Dr. Berquist," Mrs. Black said. "He has come to pray for Tina. Tina has been sick and we are going to ask Jesus to make her well. Dr. Berquist will anoint her, but first he will explain what this means."

"Boys and girls," I began, "I know that you know that Jesus loves us. If you believe this, raise your hand."

Twenty-four hands were raised.

"Well, let me tell you something about Jesus. When he was here on earth, he claimed to be a king. In fact, he claimed to be a king above all other kings. Do you know what a king is?"

"Yes," they answered, "a king can do whatever he wants. He rules over people."

103

"You are right. In Israel, when the people wanted to make someone a king, they anointed him. That is, they put oil on his head. Then everyone knew he was king.

"Now when they looked for a king that would be strong enough and wise enough to build a kingdom that would last forever, they had a name for him. The name is in the Hebrew language, which is the language that God used to write the Old Testament. Do you know what name this is?"

"No, tell us," the children spoke almost all at once.

"The name is *messiah*. That is the Hebrew word that means 'anointed.' Can you say that word with me?"

"*Messiah,*" they chanted.

"Say it again."

"*Messiah.*" It is wonderful how little children are not afraid of foreign words.

"As time moved on," I continued, "we came to New Testament days. Jesus was born. But even before he was born, God had a plan for him. He would be especially anointed.

"One day a woman talked to Jesus and told him that she and all her friends were waiting for the Messiah to come. 'When he comes,' she said, 'he will be called Christ.' *Christ* is a word in the Greek language. It means 'anointed,' in the same way as *Messiah* in the Hebrew language.

"Jesus said, 'I am the one you are looking for. I am the Christ, the Messiah.'

"This is how we know that Jesus can heal Tina today. God has anointed Jesus as king—and kings can do whatever they want. And Jesus wants to make Tina well. How many of you children believe that he does?"

Again twenty-four hands went up. Twenty-five, actually, because I raised my hand, too.

"Now there is one more thing I want to tell you about. The Bible tells us how we can anoint people, too. I am going to read it to you.

> Is any sick among you? let him call for the elders of the church; and let them pray over him, anointing him with oil in the name of the Lord: And the prayer of faith shall save the sick, and the Lord shall raise him up.
>
> —James 5:14, 15

104

"This is what I am going to do for Tina. I have a bottle of oil in my hand. In Bible times, olive oil was used because there are so many olive trees there. I am going to put some on Tina'a head. This means that I want Jesus' power to come into her body. Jesus' power is bigger than the power of sickness, any kind of sickness.

"Come over here, Tina, I am going to anoint you."

Then I asked all the children to form a circle, holding hands while I prayed. I simply asked King Jesus to take away Tina's sickness.

As I prepared to leave, several children raised their hands. "Mrs. Black, shouldn't we do something else?"

"What do you have in mind?"

"Shouldn't we thank Jesus for healing Tina?"

"Of course," I said. And we did.

As I returned to my office, I prayed another prayer of thanksgiving—thanksgiving that it is still possible to teach children of this amazing truth about Jesus.

What happened to Tina?

You shouldn't have to ask, but I am glad you did. Two days later when Tina went to the doctor for tests, we discovered that she was indeed healed. The disease was gone. And now, years later, it is still gone.

The disease? Second-grader Tina had been diagnosed as having leukemia, cancer of the blood.

Anointing has become very special to me.

My cup runneth over.
—Psalm 23:5

Chapter 20:

Not Just Adequate, But Abundant

Thus far in our study of Psalm 23, we have talked only incidentally of sheep. Fascinating as the rural life of ancient Israel may be to the serious Bible student, most of us are not excited by it. Sheep or shepherds are not a part of life today as they once were.

Tranquil fields of a distant land seem worlds away from the crises of today. Like sheep, we are frustrated, but with different concerns. I love the title of Lorraine Peterson's book for teenagers *If God Loves Me, Why Can't I Get My Locker Open?*

That book puts life in perspective. To a sixteen-year-old girl, the life of a lamb on the plains of Esdraelon is not terribly important. Actually, not even slightly important. What is important is what to do about a self-image threatened by acne and academic hassles. For her, Algebra 2 is a wolf in the badlands. A competitive sister is a more pressing problem than warble flies.

Granted, not all of us want the same things at the same time in our lives, but we all have needs. Other people's needs may seem trivial to us, but not to them.

Adults often smile condescendingly at young love and call it "puppy love." If they can recall their own youth, they may remember that even "puppy love" is very real to the puppies.

The study of Psalm 23 keeps reminding us of the progressive nature of God's leadership. We need to keep growing in response to this leadership.

In a sense, one does not simply become a Christian; he or she keeps on becoming Christian. Nothing is fatal or final if we keep following the Shepherd.

In *The Miracle and Power of Blessing* I discuss the importance of a positive attitude toward oneself. In fact, blessing oneself is the first step in blessing others.

Unfortunately, most believers discover their greatest problem is blessing themselves. They can believe that God loves them, but they find it hard to bless themselves.

Jesus, the Good Shepherd, summarized our responsibility:

> Thou shalt love the Lord thy God with all thy heart, and with all thy soul, and with all thy mind, and with all thy strength. . . . Thou shalt love thy neighbor as thyself.
>
> —Mark 12:30-31

When the mind is full of self-dislike or even hatred, it cannot pour out love on other people.

For a cup to run over, it must first be filled.

Half-empty cups trying to splash make for frantic activity, but little fulfillment. The world is full of people with a "redeemer complex." They run around putting Band-aids on the wounds of others to keep from facing their own inner hurts.

Certainly wanting to help other people is commendable, but when it is an escape from ourselves, it is dangerous. Even deadly. Not only does the would-be redeemer miss his or her own destiny, but the warped view of life actually poisons others. To minister to others out of an impoverished life is an exercise in self-destruction. Even positive thinking cannot take the place of fulfillment. Attempting to feed others from a banquet of bubbles will not work. Trying to be an overflowing person without being a fulfilled person is again futile.

God wants to fill our lives, to sing with David, "My cup runneth over." This is the way he works.

When Jesus fed the multitude with only five loaves of bread and two small fish, everyone was satisfied and the disciples gathered twelve baskets full of leftovers. When God supplies, God supplies abundantly.

Languishing in the pig pen, the prodigal son dreamed of his father's table where "even the servants have bread enough and to spare."

The Book of Malachi commands: "Bring ye all the tithes into the storehouse, that there may be meat in mine house, and prove me now herewith, saith the Lord of hosts, if I will not open you the windows of heaven, and pour you out a blessing, that there shall not be room enough to receive it" (3:10).

The New Testament echoes this:

> Give, and it shall be given unto you, good measure, pressed down, and shaken together, and running over, shall men give into your bosom.
>
> —Luke 6:38

In my study of Scripture, I cannot recall any instance in which God promises to fill anything, without also promising to make it overflow. God loves to give like that. And he wants us to do the same.

A dangerous heresy is abroad in the world today. Christians are led to believe that they are not truly "spiritual" unless they maintain a kind of desperate intensity, a sense of dissatisfaction. Setting impossible goals and then straining painfully to meet them is not necessarily an act of spiritual maturity.

God plans victory for us as we fulfill his dreams. When we strive to accomplish our own goals, or even worse, the goals others set for us, we are doomed to fail.

Life is not merely adequate but abundant when God leads.

No one would question the fact that cups come in all sizes.

People are different. Their capacities vary. But we may all be filled.

What peace this brings! The most agonizing feeling in the world is inadequacy, a sense of lack. One desperate mother cried out: "I feel like a six-piece pie being served to twelve people."

Stretching ourselves to meet others' expectations is a guaranteed formula for stress. Letting the Good Shepherd lead us is a guaranteed plan for peace of mind.

Being stressed out is becoming more and more common among Christians. Small wonder a little girl was heard to pray, "Dear God, please make all the bad people good, and, dear God, please make all the good people nice."

It's difficult to be relaxed and giving to others when we are digging the spurs in our own sides.

Having trusted the Lord during life, we have no fear of trusting him in death. If he has led us to greener pastures on this earth, it is likely he will lead us to even better things in the world to come. We shall, indeed, dwell in the house of the Lord forever.

The song "He Leadeth Me" has a personal meaning for me. Coming from Sweden as a young man, my father never learned to speak English without a pronounced accent. Whether or not this was a hindrance, I do not know. I simply know that he never acquired much in the way of wealth or position.

As a laborer for the Santa Fe Railroad, my father earned little money. His family grew until he had six children. Being the oldest boy, I watched my parents struggle to provide for us during the years of economic depression.

One of my most vivid memories is of my father trying to get one of my little brothers to sleep. He carried Johnny on his shoulder and sang to him. "He Leadeth Me" was one of his favorite songs. Since he did not think anyone was listening to him, he sang in Swedish, the language of his childhood.

> He leadeth me, O blessed thought,
> O words with heavenly comfort fraught,
> What-e'er I do, where'er I be,
> Still 'tis God's hand that leadeth me.

Years later, when I had a son of my own, I remembered. My son Marty had difficulty breathing and I had to walk the floor with him night after night. As I walked, I thought of how difficult life must have been for my parents in those days. The challenge of providing for a family on his meager pay must have been exhausting.

As I thought of those things, I was glad that my father had a Good Shepherd to lead him. Faith is born in difficult times.

In time I left home for college. The year of my graduation I was working in a factory to pay my school bills. One day a telegram came telling me that my father was seriously ill. I was needed at home.

After a long train ride, I reached Topeka, Kansas, late at night. Without stopping at our home, I went directly to the Santa Fe hospital. Even now I can recall the medicinal smell of the hospital as I walked into it and inquired for the room of Mr. Berquist. I can hear again the creaking wood floors under my feet as I walked into my father's room.

Could this be my father?

Lying on the bed, almost as white as the sheets, was the shadow of the muscular man who let us children chin ourselves on his outstretched arm. He was in a coma; he did not respond to my greeting.

I began a long watch at his bedside. I wanted to talk to him again. I wanted him to talk to me.

Hours passed. Finally he stirred. He opened his mouth as though to speak. Instead he began to sing. I recognized the words. Although sung in Swedish, the language of his boyhood, the melody was familiar. They were the words he sang as he paced the floor, carrying Johnny.

He leadeth me, O blessed thought.

And with these words he left us.

I do not know what passed through his mind in those closing moments of his life. Perhaps he recalled the difficult days of the Depression, the anxieties of rearing a family. Those are past. Now a new challenge awaits him. He stands at the crossing point of life and death. Who can see? Who can know? What faith sustains us?

The melody haunts me now. The words never leave me.

This is David's song, Psalm 23. In a sense, my father illustrated the theme of this book. Like everyone who reads this book, he is a special person. And, the *I* that he was he still IS. He lives. And the fact that my father belonged to the Lord in life, I know that he is still HIS.

What a comfort this is.

As you opened this book, you may have noticed that it was lovingly dedicated to Mary and Joe Minkler. Mary and Joe have walked through the valley of the shadow of death many times. Not only was their young son killed in a motorcycle accident, but a long and debilitating disease took the life of Everett, Joe's brother. Beloved parents have been taken by death. As I have written about my father, I think of Mary and Joe and of many other friends who have passed through difficult places.

To those who have been led by the Good Shepherd, there is little in this book that is amazing. The stories I have told will be much the same as theirs, only the names will be changed. To those who have not yet asked the Lord to lead them, a truly amazing world awaits.

To all of those who read these lines, I hope that when they walk in dark places, God's word will become a lamp to their feet and a light to their path.

To all who are imprisoned by sickness, frustration, or sin, I offer hope. David has given us a song to sing. Let us sing it and share it.

The Good Shepherd has led me to Psalm 23 and Psalm 23 has led me to the Good Shepherd. And I am thankful.

Surely goodness and mercy shall follow me all the days of my life: and I will dwell in the house of the Lord forever."
—Psalm 23:6

Chapter 21:

We May Change Sheepfolds, But We Never Change Shepherds

An overflowing life leaves behind it a trail of blessing. Goodness and mercy follow.

In the world of sheep we see that, properly led, sheep not only are nourished, but they nourish the pastures on which they feed. A careless or lazy shepherd will allow sheep to overgraze the land until it is wasted. Not only do the sheep suffer, but the land itself may never recover.

Carefully tended sheep are known as "those with the golden hooves." Not only do they keep moving on to new pastures so they do not exhaust the earth, but their droppings enrich the soil. Even barren, rutted fields have been revitalized by careful management of the sheep.

The earthy illustration reminds us that properly led, Christians leave a trail of blessing behind them. Even when they are passing through difficult times, they leave things better than they found them.

In another of his psalms, David speaks of people like this:

> Who passing through the valley of Baca make it a well;
> the rain also filleth up the pools. They go from strength
> to strength . . . in Zion.
>
> —Psalm 84:6, 7

The valley of Baca was a place of desolation. It represents all the hardships through which we must pass. But when unplanned problems arise, we may either bless them or curse them. We may solve the problem and thus leave a blessing behind us when we move on to future goals.

How much poorer we would be if Paul had not been imprisoned. The Romans were not good to him, but goodness followed him. In a dark and damp cell, Paul lit a torch that lights our path and warms our hearts.

In our day, Joni Eareckson Tada is a testimony of residual goodness. Paralyzed by a swimming accident, Joni learned that the Good Shepherd could lead her through the dark valley of frustrated dreams and plans. Not only has she survived, but an aura of goodness follows her.

Mercy, too, should follow believers. Since all of us have received mercy from the Good Shepherd, we must in turn show mercy to others. "All we like sheep have gone astray," Isaiah tells us. Therefore, when we encounter others who are straying, we can afford to be merciful.

Like sheep, humans follow their instincts to dangerous places. The Good Shepherd's staff pulls us back, even when we resist. He pours healing oil into our wounds. Whether we are bleeding from our own disobedience or by attacks from wild animals, God is merciful.

What a delicious feeling to experience the mercy of God. Only one emotion surpasses it: being merciful to others.

Mercy precedes us in salvation.
Mercy restores us as God forgives us.
Mercy follows us as we forgive others.

114

With these words we come to the end of David's sweet song. We began with the Lord as our Shepherd, and we end with the Lord still being our shepherd. After a lifetime of following our Shepherd, the good news is that when death comes, we do not change shepherds, we merely change sheepfolds. We are still led.

Printed in the United States
49619LVS00002B/436-444